Somewhere Along the Way

A collection of selected essays, poems and short stories

By Richard Standring

ISBN 9-781591-964872

Somewhere Along the Way

Published Work

Hustle (Electronic Media) 1989

Dangerous Dancing (Xlibris) 1999

Dangerous Relationships (Infinity) 2001

Dangerous Encounters (Infinity) 2003

Vanished (This short story appears in an anthology, *Stories of the Unexpected*) 2004

Note: All the poems appearing here can also be seen on the Internet www.poetry.com and have appeared in various editions published by the International Poetry Society. All the short stories are works of fiction and do not reflect any known persons. Most of the places exist, however, some may have a fictitious name.

A special thanks to all my friends in the Cookeville Creative Writer's Assoc. who encouraged me and provided a good forum for critiques; something every writer needs to move forward. I appreciate your listening to my stories and all your suggestions.
RAS

Richard Standring

Contents

Essays: Page:

A Special Place	153
Alligators	27
Ask Your Doctor About...	161
Corporate Doublespeak & Other Lies	49
Early Lessons	157
I'll Tell You What...	131
Legends, Myths, Folktales & Spooky Stuff	93
Of Days Gone By	111
The Pitchman's Dance	87

Poems:

Bragging About the South	139
Crackistan	85
Rattlesnake Bend	47
Remnants	37
River Dreaming	63
Shiloh	109
The Storyteller's Tale	7

Short Stories:

A Distant Drum	101
Bad Day at Flat Rock	53
Do the Math	162
Ghost Diner on Rt. 12	29
Gigolo Sunset	65
Incident at Hillside Elementary	39
Passing Through Rugby	23
The Art of Winning	141
The Dixie	43
The Men's Room	123
The Night the Canaries Wailed on High St.	9
What Tomorrow Brings	97
Where the Sun Always Shines	135

Somewhere Along the Way

Richard Standring

Forward

Thoughts, daydreams and ideas for stories come together over time. Sometimes an idea comes to me while I'm driving. Several of the poems and short stories presented here were written some time ago. Remnants was written in 1967 as a tribute to my father and the first airport he created from a farm. Later, through the magic of osmosis, some of his dreams became my dreams, too. When I became a pilot, I came to know the skies he loved and the mystery of all the strange places below. The rest of the stories were added later. Most are the byproduct of traveling and meeting interesting people **along the way**. A few stories are reflections of the past, as I remember it.

The essays allow me to express my opinions on the human condition and unusual elements of life. Some are observations, others just fond memories.

Like all human drama, there is some humor and a little sadness. It is fiction and fantasy, with threads of truth woven here and there to be entertaining.

Some of the poems are reflections of a given moment. All for you to enjoy and ponder as you travel along with me on an imaginative path. **Somewhere along the way**, I found a magic microscope, or maybe it was a telescope, that has allowed me to view life from a slightly different perspective. Like the storyteller's kaleidoscope of life, the view keeps changing.

Richard A. Standring

Somewhere Along the Way

Richard Standring

The Storyteller's Tale

I've done my daring do,
And dreams, I've had a few.
Before the day is through,
I'll tell you one or two.

I recall I was a stranger,
Traveling in a faraway land.
There were lots of palm trees,
Miles and miles of sand.

There was a time when I would fly.
Sometimes low, sometimes high.
The land below, a patchwork maze.
I still remember those days.

Some stories just might bore you,
Others may not be quite true.
I'll save some for another day,
As storytellers like to do.

Someday you'll tell your stories,
Some dreams never came true.
Still quite an adventure, eh?
It becomes part of you.

RAS

Somewhere Along the Way

Richard Standring

The Night the Canaries Wailed on High Street

A humorous short story about the patrons of a hillbilly bar in a fictitious old town, located somewhere on the Ohio River.

Dad always said, "If you're alone in a strange town, find an old hillbilly bar, and you'll pass the evening with some interesting new friends". Now Dad was a bit of a drinker, and he sure had his fair share of friends. Most were drinking buddies. Years later, I was thinking about some of his offbeat wisdom while passing through an old river town in southern Ohio. Port Avery is about a hundred miles east of Cincinnati, and about sixty years behind the present.

High Street, in Port Avery, runs north & south. The south end stops at a small park overlooking the Ohio River. There are several restored old mansions at this end of town before you get to the commercial area. A few blocks north of Main, High Street slowly rises deteriorating along the way. Many of the stores in this section of town have fallen on hard times. Those that have remained in business, exhibit faded signs, dirty windows and old dusty merchandise.

Billy's Bar is at the top of High Street, sandwiched between two empty stores. Across the street is an old laundromat and a vacant lot. If the weeds were cut down on the lot, you would have a nice view of the town below, and part of the river. Because of its location, the locals call it "Billy's on the Hill". The clientele would indicate that the name was *almost* appropriate. It was the kind of watering hole Dad would have investigated.

Billy's has two neon beer signs, one in each front

Somewhere Along the Way

window, projecting the only spot of color on the entire block after dark. It's also the only entertainment in the area, such as it is. Old country-western tunes blare from a '50s juke box in the rear from 2:00 in the afternoon until closing. After midnight, Billy obliges the neighbors by closing the front door, to keep the sound partially contained.

Official closing time is 2:00 AM, at which point the remaining drunks are pushed out the door and sent home. For many, Billy's Bar is their home away from home.

Blind Bob is one of the regulars who arrives around 4:00 in the afternoon for his first drink of the day. Earlier in the day, he can be found sitting outside the bus station selling pencils. Sitting beside him is Arlo, a big black Labrador whose only mission is to be Blind Bob's constant companion. Blind Bob always occupies the sixth bar stool from the front door at Billy's, putting him close to the middle of the room. Six is supposed to be his lucky number, and sometimes represents the number of beers he'll drink before he and Arlo leave. It really depends on who's buying. The sixth bar stool also happens to be the only stool without some sort of tear in the red plastic covering.

Five booths in various stages of disrepair grace the wall opposite the bar. The gray Formica tabletops display 40 year's worth of cigarette burns and scratches. All the seats were covered in red vinyl at one time, to match the bar stools. It's a safe bet that Billy hasn't spent a nickel on fixing up the place in the past ten years, which is okay with the locals who patronize the place. If you asked them, they wouldn't change a thing.

Billy's is open seven days a week, and I suspect most of the locals show up every day, listening to the same old music, drinking the same drinks, and rehashing old arguments that seem to continue like a TV soap opera. There's not that much to talk about in Port Avery, particularly for those who are retired, or unemployed. That makes up 95 per cent of all the locals at Billy's.

Blind Bob represents part of the remaining five per cent who have something to do during the earlier part of the day. Behind the bar, B.J. (short for Barbara Jean) has the task of opening bottles and cans, washing a few glasses and mixing drinks. Most of the mixed drinks are rum and coke, seven and seven, or peach schnapps on the rocks. At least a dozen of the bottles on the back bar are half full and have remained that way for over a year, collecting dust. Billy's is one of the few remaining bars where a shot of rye whiskey is still 50 cents. Draft beer is 60 cents, when the tap is working, and cans are 75 cents. The selection of beer is limited to three brands, one of which are advertised in neon in the front windows. All the patrons know the rules, and the menu of limited offerings.

The rules are noted on the wall above the cash register saving B.J. a lot of needless conversation:

1. No Credit & No bar tabs. Pay when served.
2. Only Billy & B.J. allowed behind the bar.
3. No fancy drinks served.
4. Don't sit in Blind Bob's seat. #6
5. No shoes, no shirt, no service, no shit!
6. You better be 21, or a very good liar.

Those are the rules at Billy's Bar, at the top of High Street, in Port Avery. As a complete stranger in town, with a few hours to kill on a hot summer afternoon, I happened onto Billy's. I managed to break rule number four first, then rule three soon after.

"We ain't got any Coors Lite," B.J., the barmaid said. "And if we did, I wouldn't give you any, 'cause you're sittin' in Blind Bob's seat. You'd best move over one, and leave some room for Arlo," B.J. looked to be in her late forties, but it was really hard to judge her age.

She reminded me of one of those tired, overworked women who didn't know how to smile, or had forgotten how. Like some of the others already getting their day started here, she had false teeth, along with the telltale caved-in cheeks, and an accent. I noticed earlier that many of the women in this part of the country looked older than they probably were. Maybe it was the hard life they lived. Many of the coal mining towns had people like that. Most of the locals at Billy's looked to be on welfare, or collecting Social Security.

Sitting in a booth directly behind me was a big, heavy woman wearing a faded housedress and slippers. Her dyed black hair had gray roots showing. Across from her sat the skinniest man I'd ever seen. He wore a dirty undershirt, jeans, old sneakers and a railroader's cap. Most of his teeth were missing. Neither of them talked. He just tapped his hand on the table to the music and they nodded at each other.

I was surprised to see anyone in the bar this early. B.J. kept herself busy lighting one cigarette after another, leaving it to get someone a drink, then lighting another. While she may have forgotten where she left her lit cigarette, she always knew who had ordered a drink, and never forgot to collect for it.

I was starting on my second beer when Blind Bob arrived. He tapped his white cane on the floor more as an announcement of his arrival, than a testing for obstructions. He knew every square inch of the place, and all the locals. He called them "reglars". This was a place where "Y'all" and "You'ens" was acceptable along with "prolly" (an unofficial contraction for probably). In this atmosphere, I was the only person out of place. On B.J.'s instructions, I had moved over to the next bar stool, prior to Blind Bob's arrival.

Blind Bob sat at his spot at the bar, making sure Arlo was sitting next to him. Then he turned to me and said, "You musta been sittin' here in my seat." It was more of a statement than a direct question. His dark glasses stared at me and I felt compelled to say something.

"Yes, I'm sorry. The barmaid wouldn't serve me while I sat there. How did you know?" I replied.

"Seat's still warm. Only a stranger would sit here, ain't that right, Arlo?" With that, the big black Lab gave out with a "Woooff" acknowledging his master's question.

"What brings you to Port Avery? We don't see many new people around here."

Blind Bob was staring at the mirror on the wall behind the dusty whiskey bottles. There was no need for him to face me even though I was turned toward him. I was trying to determine his age and settled on mid-fifties. He needed a shave and a haircut. His frame was on the bony side of thin, and the fingers on his right hand displayed nicotine stains. As soon as he was seated, B.J. had placed a can of beer in front of him. He in turn had placed three quarters and a half empty pack of Marlboro's on the counter. B.J. left with the money without a word being said between them. I was witnessing their daily ritual.

"Here on business, just for the day," I replied. The truth was, I was curious about the town and had some time to kill. After walking around in the sun, I decided on this quaint old place for a drink. Actually the music drew my attention to it. I'm a Willie Nelson fan.

"Can I buy you a drink?" I asked.

He was half way through his first beer. He drank from the can, B.J. hadn't brought him a glass. It probably simplified finding his drink on the bar. A glass would be just one more thing to get in the way, and B.J. looked like she didn't want to wash any more glasses than absolutely necessary.

"Sure. You can buy Arlo one, too."

Without waiting for me to respond, he called B.J. over and told her I was buying him and Arlo a round. In less time than it took to give her the order, she was back with two beers. One she placed in front of Blind Bob, the other, she popped open and poured into a small dirty-looking bowl she pushed toward Arlo. The dog moved to the bowl and began lapping at the beer. I decided he must have been exceptionally thirsty.

"He sure seems to like beer," I mused, as I put money on the bar for B.J. who was patiently waiting.

"Makes him fart a lot," Blind Bob chuckled, holding up his beer as an acknowledgment of thanks. Later, I began to suspect it was a rallying signal for all the free loaders.

"Musta got up to at least eighty-seven here today," he said to no one in particular. And since no one answered him, I decided to ask a question. I had seen the thermometer reading on a sign at the bank an hour earlier indicating that precise temperature, which was

13

about right for late June.
"How did you happen to know exactly how hot it was today?" I knew blind people had sharper senses, but this had me puzzled.
"Heard it on the radio a while ago." He said it so matter-of-factly that I instantly felt foolish. "That's okay, everyone thinks being blind, leaves you minus some brain tissue, too. Well, it just ain't so. I can tell you who everyone is here in the bar right now, and just where they're sittin' or standin'." I had the feeling I was being had again, but it didn't really matter. He was an interesting character, and someone to pass the time with.
"Yes, I'll bet you can... with the exception of me."
"Yeah, well why don't you tell me yer name so I'll know you next time you're here."
"My name's Daniel, but everyone just calls me Danny, or Dan."
"Oh Danny Boy, the pipes, the pipes are call...ing. From glen to glen and down the mountain side...." Blind Bob was singing the song slightly off-key. "That's about all I can remember," he said, "but it sure used to bring tears to my eyes. I changed my first name to Bob. Real name's Rupert. Middle name's Robert, that's where the Bob comes from."
"How long have you been blind, Bob?"
"Been blind most of my life. Been sightless for the last fifteen years." The man's wit wasn't wasted on me. I quickly determined Bob was a lot more intelligent than he first appeared. It was a common mistake for a stranger like me to make.
"Well, when you put it that way, I guess we all have our blind spots." It was a wasted pun. I was beginning to feel relaxed and unbuttoned my collar and loosened my tie.
"In here, you sure don't need a tie." Blind Bob continued to stare at the mirror, so I was surprised he would even know that I was wearing a tie, since he hadn't touched me.
"Why don't you tell me what color it is?" I decided to test him a little.
"If you want to play games, it's okay with me, but

it'll cost you another beer."

"Okay, but no more for Arlo. Because that'd be contributing to the delinquency of a canine," I chuckled at my own joke. B.J. giggled.

"Hear that, Arlo? The man here called you a dirty name."

With that, Arlo growled softly. I was beginning to wonder if the pooch understood what we were talking about? Blind Bob tapped the empty can in front of him calling out to B.J. "Another one over here, Hon." The man sure drank fast!

"You haven't guessed the color of my tie yet."

"How many chances do I get?"

"Just one. That was the bet."

"Okay, it's red." B.J. had already served him another beer and was waiting for me to pay her. No tabs in this establishment. It said so in the rules hanging on the wall, just above the cash register.

"I'll be damned! How did you know that?" I was truly amazed that a blind man would know I was wearing a dark red silk tie with very light blue stripes. He hadn't mentioned the light blue stripes, nor did I expect him to.

"Danny Boy, when you're in my condition, and broke all the time, you learn ways to get things. The longer you sit here, and if you keep buyin' drinks, you'll see a lot of interesting things goin' on 'round here. Take Susie over there for example...." He motioned with his left hand, not turning toward the front booth where a young woman, with bleached blond hair, sat facing a much older man with a face full of wrinkles.

She was in her early twenties, the man could be anywhere from early forties to early sixties. He was wearing a ball cap and smoking one cigarette after another while trying to console the young woman. He kept reaching across the table patting her hand. I couldn't hear what they were saying. She appeared to be crying.

"So what's Susie's problem?" I asked. The man she was with could have been her father, or even her grandfather.

"Susie's doin' her routine. Comes in here cryin' that her old man threw her out without any money, hopin' someone will give her a few bucks, or buy her a drink. She tries to trick 'em into thinkin' she needs a place to stay, too."

"Well, if they're all locals, aren't they aware of her routine?"

"Oh sure. It's a game. They all play it, just like that music. Same old shit night after night. Susie's girl friend, Wanda Lee, will be along shortly. And she'll start hustlin' for quarters for the jukebox. Then she'll start dancin' and movin' around. She's got some pretty good moves left in her. Used to be a stripper in one of them topless bars outside of town. Nice tits, but her belly has gotten too fat along with her ass."

I wondered how he knew, but didn't ask.

"Those two, along with Gloria, are a bunch of canaries," he added reaching for his cigarettes.

"Canaries?" I didn't understand.

"Yeah, that's what I call 'em. They all got bleached blond hair, and they're all the time hustlin' for drinks and moochin' cigarettes. And singin' out of tune with that music box Billy's got back there. You'll see. Except Gloria ain't here no more. She died a few days ago. That's prolly what got Susie so upset. They were pretty close."

"This Gloria, how'd she die?"

"Died right here. Fell off a bar stool over there and hit her head on the floor."

"And that killed her?"

"No, I didn't say *the fall* killed her. Actually, the paper said she had a massive heart attack, so she might have been dead by the time she hit the floor. Who knows? Dead is dead anyway."

"Were you here when it happened?"

"'Course I was. Saw the whole damned thing."

I wondered if that was an innocent slip? Maybe everyone in here was a con artist, including Blind Bob. After all, he'd already gotten into me for a few beers. And Arlo, was he just a prop for the con job, too? I was having some doubts, but enjoying the shabby atmosphere just the same. Most of the patrons seemed to be listening to other conversations, or the music. Susie got up and passed by me on her way to the toilet in the back,

Richard Standring

by the jukebox and pay telephone. I watched her all the way to the rear, admiring her small, cute ass in faded cut-offs.

"Cute ass, huh?" Blind Bob was smiling into the mirror and looking smug, like he'd read my mind. "I like it when she doesn't wear a bra, like tonight. Those little bitty nipples she's got push out just enough to tease you."

"How... how did you know she wasn't wearing a bra?"

"'Cause she never wears one," he laughed. In a few minutes she returned brushing by Blind Bob and poking him in the ribs. He reached out and encircled her waist with his right arm bringing her close to him.

"Susie, say hello to Danny Boy here."

"It's Dan," I reminded him.

"Hello Danny Boy here," she giggled. "Is *here* your last name?" We all laughed at this old corny joke.

"She calls all the men, 'Hon' don't you, Love?" I noticed that Blind Bob's hand had worked its way up to just under her right breast before she pulled away. He still managed to pat her on the behind. Being blind must have allowed him a few liberties with the ladies. And he obviously took them.

"You gonna buy me a drink, Hon?" She was starting to cry and for no apparent reason. "My best friend just died. She was my very best friend in the whole world. Now she's dead. I'm not sure I can handle that right now, so I'm gonna get good and drunk tonight before I go over to Raspberry's to see her laid out."

As if on cue, B.J. was there with a rum & coke, or at least that's what it looked like. "That'll be a dollar, Hon." Now even B.J. was calling me 'Hon'. I was beginning to feel like a regular. Susie took a long swallow of her drink, sat the glass down in front of Blind Bob and started to dance, by herself, to the music. She must have fed the jukebox on her way back from the toilet. Susie had a lost look on her face as she swayed to the music. She seemed to be focusing on the old tin tile ceiling.

A few seconds passed and an older man sitting down the bar got up and started to dance with her. He looked a little silly, because he was moving his hips from side to side at a different tempo than Susie, or the music.

Somewhere Along the Way

Looking around the bar, couples sitting in the booths watched without any expression. They had seen it all before, hundreds of times. To me, they all looked like mannequins. At the moment, Susie was their only entertainment.

There was some commotion at the front of the bar, near the entrance. "Must be Wanda Lee's arrived." Blind Bob was stating another of his timely facts, which I now no longer questioned. Looking toward the door, I could see a blond woman standing between two men at the bar. I couldn't hear what was said for the increasing noise level. Wanda Lee was another bleached blond about the same height as Susie, they were each just a little over five feet tall. Susie was trim and maybe weighed 100 lbs. where Wanda Lee was twice her weight. Her figure was accented by teased hair. It gave her head a big balloon appearance. She wore heavy make-up and chewed gum. She was hugging and kissing several of the older men sitting near the entrance.

"Don't give her any money," Blind Bob whispered.
"Why would I do that?"
"Because sooner or later, she'll ask you for some."
"She doesn't even know me, or that I'm here."
"Oh she will in time. She's just workin' her way down the line. Good for a few free feels, but she don't put out. She'll let you think different though."

"Part of the game, right?" I was catching on. And Blind Bob was showing me how it was. This was a sub-culture, foreign to me until today.

"You got it. Good time for you to go to the toilet and count yer money. Put half in one pocket, and half someplace else, like yer sock. That way, you won't lose it all."

"Why are you telling me to do that?"
"Why? So you'll be able to buy drinks. Me and Arlo here got us a good thing goin' tonight don't we, Arlo?"
"Woooff"

When I returned from the men's room, which was a unique experience, there were fresh beers sitting on the bar, and B.J. waiting with a big smile. The first I'd seen from her.

"Dan, do you remember those old knock, knock

jokes we used to tell years ago?" Blind Bob turned to me as I sat down. I just nodded my head without saying a word. He continued, "Well I got one for you. Ready?" Again, I just nodded.
"Knock, knock...."
"Okay, who's there," I felt silly.
"Yaa...."
"Yaa? Yaa who?" I played along.
"Yaa Hoo! Don't say that too loud or someone in here might think you're a cowboy." Suddenly there were several others laughing with Blind Bob. It was enough to bring Wanda Lee down on a search mission. She was scowling.

"How can you guys be laughing when Glory is going to her grave tomorrow!" She admonished us with hands on her wide hips. Her hips flared into thunder thighs. Wanda Lee was big in the rear, too. If she lost 60 pounds she might look halfway decent. Right now, she could pass for a lady wrestler, or do double duty as a bouncer. Either way, I guessed she could be trouble without much provocation.

"Danny Boy here didn't know Gloria, so bag it, Wanda Lee. We all feel bad about what happened. After all, Gloria was queen of the canaries around here."

"Oh yeah? You plannin' on goin' over to Raspberry's later with the rest of us? I hear they got her laid out real nice and natural-lookin."

"I don't know yet. Maybe I will, and then, maybe I'll just sit here in the peace and quiet, knowing the joint will be empty for a change. And I won't hafta listen to all yer screamin' and yellin'." Blind Bob spoke to the mirror reaching for another cigarette.

"Don't be a smart ass with me, Bob, or I'll knock you off that bar stool so fast...." before she could finish, Arlo was standing up and softly growling. He sensed that something had changed and was ready to defend Bob, who unconcerned, reached down to pat his head.

"Now see what you just did? You got Arlo all pissed off. You make a move on me, you fat bitch, and Arlo here will take a bite out of your big fat ass!"

"Stop it, just stop it!" cried Susie breaking into the confrontation. "Glory's gone, and she's all I had. She was like a big sister to me." Susie was crying again, and it looked like Wanda Lee might soften up any moment.

"There, there, Baby. Hang on now." Wanda Lee had her arms wrapped around Susie hugging her. In the background, some cowboy was singing a song about makin' it through the night. Both women were crying now, and everyone at the bar was trying to buy them a drink. It would have been Gloria's finest hour, had she been there. According to Blind Bob, she was queen of the bar flies, and could hustle drinks with the best of them.

"It's gonna be some wake!" Blind Bob said stubbing out a cigarette and lighting another. "All these drunks in here, goin' over to Raspberry's funeral parlor to see Gloria laid out in a yellow dress. You can bet they're gonna' embarrass Gloria's folks, and anyone else who's sober. Oh it'll be a night to remember alright!"

"I don't give a shit who likes it, I'm goin'," said Susie overhearing Blind Bob's comment. "Maybe I'll even get drunk enough to kill myself and go with her, what do you think of that?" Several men were trying to console her while patting her on the shoulder, and her behind.

"If yer gonna pay yer last respects to Glory, you better get right with God, first." One of the men stated, followed by a loud, long belch. It reminded me of a Foster Brooks routine. I expected him to fart next.

"If I know Glory, she's already hustlin' Jesus for a pack of smokes," someone else added with a giggle.

"They don't allow smokin' in Heaven," another said.

"Oh yeah, how do you know?" Another argument was about to erupt. Blind Bob was holding up his empty beer can for B.J. to bring him a replacement, not putting any money on the bar now. I was expected to pay for the privilege of witnessing all that had happened so far.

"I just know, okay? God don't allow any of that shit to happen. You can't drink up there, you can't swear and you can't smoke. It says so in the Bible," Susie yelled.

"Don't think Glory's gonna be too happy then." Comments were coming from everywhere. Blind Bob smiled at the new interest everyone seemed to be showing. It was all because of Gloria. She had been the main entertainment here. Susie and Wanda Lee were her able assistants, rubbing the backs of the old men at the bar, hoping they'd get a free drink. And maybe *borrow* a few dollars, which would never be repaid.

"If I know Glory, she's gonna sneak a few packs in with her." One toothless old gent offered, giggling again, "and ask Jesus for a light!"

Susie and Wanda Lee were crying in a high-pitched wail, giving it everything they had. They were surrounded by a half dozen old-timers. Each one trying to console them with friendly body pats. It looked like a football huddle.

I decided it was time to leave and edged around the mourners, such as they were. I left a five-dollar tip on the bar and noticed Blind Bob quickly snatch it.

"See ya 'round, Danny Boy," Blind Bob called after me as I reached the door. I waved as I left.

On the way home, I thought about the events of that strange afternoon and evening. Did Blind Bob deliberately not mention the blue stripes on my tie? His name for the girls, *canaries,* was certainly appropriate. And for Gloria, that evening was a fitting wake... with all her friends at Billy's, remembering her, as they knew her. Could anyone ever expect a more fitting eulogy? What a send off!

Two years have passed since that eventful trip to Port Avery and Billy's Bar on High Street. Once again I was in Cincinnati on business. I finished early and drove to Port Avery, wondering if Blind Bob would remember me? Billy's Bar was still there. It looked just as sad as the first time I saw it, driving up to the top of High Street. The view of the Ohio River was still partially blocked by tall weeds in the vacant lot across the street.

My first surprise was B.J. wasn't behind the bar. Then I noticed the sixth bar stool was missing! A square piece of thin plywood was fastened over the holes in the floor. When I asked about Blind Bob, the woman behind the bar told me he'd died of cancer several months earlier. Arlo was living with B.J. The missing bar stool was Billy's silent tribute to Blind Bob. The sign over the

Somewhere Along the Way

cash register was still there, but rule number four had a line drawn through it. She mentioned that Blind Bob and Billy were actually second cousins.

I had one beer and raised the can to the dirty mirror in a salute to Blind Bob. I remembered him trying to sing, "Oh Danny Boy" to me. The only other person who ever sang that song to me was my father when I was six years old. The memory of that brought a lump to my throat. I had to swallow hard.

I also thought about the *canaries*, and how they must have wailed at Blind Bob's wake. In a strange way, I'd had an early preview.

End

Richard Standring

Passing Through Rugby

Rugby, Tennessee is a registered historic village situated on Highway 52, close to the Big South Fork National Park, and about 25 miles east of Jamestown. It was founded in 1880 as an experimental English colony and has retained the architecture of that period. It is surrounded by thousands of acres of forest. On a clear day, the view of the mountains along the Cumberland Plateau presents a wonderful panorama, particularly in late fall when the leaves are changing color.

Rugby also happens to be situated on an invisible line that separates the eastern and central time zones.

One late October afternoon, I was driving along Highway 52, on my way home from a trip. On several other occasions I've stopped at the quaint Harrow Road Café for coffee and a snack. The food there is delicious and the atmosphere is pleasing, taking you back to an earlier time. The sign out front announces *Good Eating*. The café is situated about a hundred feet back from the highway, providing extra parking space. The stretch of road, passing through Rugby, is known as Central Ave. Several ornate homes, located on a road behind the café, offer Bed and Breakfast accommodations. I was anticipating a short rest stop and snack at the café as I approached the Morgan County line from the east.

As so often happens, the day after Daylight Savings Time disappears, dusk rapidly transitions to dark much earlier, to my chagrin. It had been raining most of the day and fog was beginning to appear in low wisps. I turned on my headlights just in time to see the sign announcing Rugby. Suddenly, the two-lane asphalt road I was on vanished! I was now driving on what appeared to be a two-lane dirt path. I hadn't noticed any construction signs posted. I immediately slowed to 25 miles per hour and paid close attention for any

Somewhere Along the Way

oncoming traffic. Thankfully there was none. As soon as I saw the small Episcopal Church on my right, I knew the café would be close by on my left. Sure enough, I found it in the diminishing light.

I noticed flickering lanterns beside the doorway and thought about the welcoming charm their soft glow added. I'd never noticed the lanterns before. However, I'd never passed this way after dark, either. I thought the lanterns were a nice authentic touch. As I parked the car, a horse-drawn buggy pulled up beside me. An older man wearing a white, long-sleeve shirt, buttoned to the top, a vest, black trousers and wide brimmed hat emerged. I noticed he was also wearing high top black shoes that laced all the way up. At first glance one might mistake them for boots. For a moment, I wondered if he might be Amish, but he was clean-shaven.

"Hello," I said. "I like your costume." I knew there was a fall festival sometime around Halloween and thought perhaps he was part of the local attraction.

"Howdy, I like yours, also," he replied tipping his hat to reveal a full head of white hair. "What is that contraption?" he asked, pointing to my automobile.

"Some people think of it as a time machine," I said. "It saves time by transporting me from one place to another quickly." Surely he knew what it was. However, he was playing his role well, just like the weekend occupants at Plymouth Plantation, another much older authentic recreation just outside Plymouth, Massachusetts.

"And where do you hale from?" He asked.

"I'm on my way home to Cookeville," I answered. "I should make it back in about an hour and half I guess."

"That so? I reckon it to be a two-day journey from here. Been there once to buy a team of mules. Too many people to suit me."

"Yes, it is growing." As we approached the doorway, I held the door open for him to enter, but he backed away motioning for me to enter first.

"No, Sir. Visitors first. That's the way it is here. No offense meant." I nodded my thanks. It felt a bit strange to have an older gentleman hold the door open for me.

Inside, a hostess greeted us with a cheery smile.

She was also in costume wearing a long gingham skirt that went to the top of her shoes. She wore a white bib apron. Her hair was pulled back in a bun. The chill of the evening vanished when I wandered over to the huge fireplace in the dining room. A fire was burning producing a pleasant fragrance and adding to the room's atmosphere. It reminded me of Williamsburg. More flickering wall lanterns added to the charm, but I had difficulty reading the menu on the chalkboard fastened to the wall by the entrance to the dining room.

When I said I wasn't staying for dinner, but would like some coffee, the waitress made an alternate suggestion.

"Perhaps you'd like some of our hot cider to warm you up. And I could bring you a nice hot biscuit with some of our homemade apple butter."

How could I refuse? I thought I might use the toilet and wash my hands before my snack arrived. As I walked into the hallway I became confused. I heard someone say, "It's out back behind the kitchen." I suspected the man who was motioning to the rear of the building meant an outhouse. If so, I could wait. I wondered why the toilet off the hallway wasn't in use as I returned to my seat and for the next few minutes enjoyed the aroma of cinnamon and spiced cider. The large biscuit was delicious, the best I'd ever eaten.

As I attempted to pay my check, the waitress announced that the older gentleman I came in with insisted on paying, since I was a visitor to the area. I waved to him as I left.

"Stop back again and stay a while," he called out.

As I left the village, I couldn't help feeling I had been transported back in time. Everything was just the way it would have been in 1880 when the village originated. There was another horse-drawn wagon outside the dry goods store adjacent to the café. Once outside the village, the dirt road disappeared and the asphalt highway suddenly reappeared. The darkness was sprinkled with distant lights from houses along the road. A big truck passed me confirming that I was back in the present.

Later that evening, I hesitated then reluctantly told

my wife about what had happened earlier as I passed through Rugby. I was sure she'd think I was daydreaming and got caught up in my own fantasy. It wasn't unlike me to do that.

"Leave it to you and that crazy imagination of yours," she said. "You've been watching too much television." It was something a parent might have said to a child who had related a wild dream.

A month later, I was once again on Highway 52 passing through Rugby. I planned for another stop at the Harrow Road Café. I could practically taste the hot cider as I approached the front door. The first thing I noticed was the outside light fixture. It was an electric lamp, not a lantern. Inside, I looked for the huge fireplace on the far wall in the dining room. I anticipated a nice warming fire, but the fireplace wasn't in the same place, and there was no fire burning.

"What happened to the fireplace that was on that wall?" I asked, pointing to the wall across the room.

"Well as you can see, Hon, it hasn't been there in years. I'm told they tore it down when they remodeled this place, but that was before my time. I'm surprised you knew there was ever one over there," the waitress said, waiting for me to order.

"Just a wild guess," I replied. I tried to hide my sudden disappointment and ordered coffee with a piece of pumpkin pie. I would have preferred some hot, spiced cider and another biscuit with apple butter.

Rugby is still a quaint historical village worth visiting, but you should have seen it before they had automobiles and electricity. It was really a neat place. I keep wondering if the time change had anything to do with my mental flash back to an earlier time. If so, I'd like to go back and do it again. Maybe when the time changes this coming spring.

End

Richard Standring

Alligators on the Interstate

Imagine a situation where you're driving 65 to 70 mph on the Interstate. There are trucks on both sides, you're in the middle lane and there's a car in front of you. So you're boxed in and everyone is moving along at the same speed.

Suddenly the car in front of you swerves to avoid something. Blam! That something is a big, long, black object and it's too late to maneuver around it. It hit's the grill and hood of your car with a loud thump causing you to flinch. In the rearview mirror you see what looks like a piece of truck tire floating between two lanes, awaiting its next unsuspecting victim.

Once you're able to stop, and survey the damage, you can see the grill is broken and there's a big dent in the hood. There could be some other damage under the car that you can't see, like a dent in the oil pan, or a bent tie rod. Later, when you're talking to a mechanic, you learn that you're lucky the piece of rubber you hit didn't break the windshield and cause even more damage. Still the price for that experience will run about $1,500 and tie up the car for two days, an added inconvenience. Even with insurance, it's going to be a significant expense.

"Those alligators will get you every time if you're not careful," the mechanic says. That's when you learn the road name for that dangerous piece of shredded truck tire. It's an *alligator*, an appropriate name.

I've seen these pieces of rubber lying beside many highways and often wondered why there were so many blown truck tires. Most of them seem to be four to six feet in length. Since my expensive experience, I've become a more wary driver. I maintain a decent distance behind the vehicle in front of me so I have time to avoid any surprises. And I try not to allow myself to

Somewhere Along the Way

get boxed in by trucks on either side, however there are times when it can't be avoided.

I was never fond of the *alligators* that live in swamps and I absolutely hate the ones that occupy space on major highways and Interstates. I also wonder how many of those monsters are the remains of cheap recaps? If that's the main source, then perhaps they should either be outlawed, or have a limited expected life on the road. While that view may anger some truckers, I submit not one trucker volunteered to help pay for my repairs.

Now that I know what an *alligator* is, what shall we call those pieces of gravel that suddenly strike the windshield leaving a star-shaped chink? Maybe we could call them *meteorites*, or *road rockets*.

End

Richard Standring

Ghost Diner on Rt. 12

If you've ever traveled along Route 12 in Michigan, between Ann Arbor and Niles, then you know this is one of the more scenic roads in the state. There's lots of small towns, lots of trees, and not too much traffic. At one time, it must have been one of the main East/West highways linking Detroit and South Bend. That would have been before the interstate was built. Part of this road passes through a place known as "Irish Hills", an area of small lakes, summer homes and a few aging amusement parks.

My name is Jerry Johnson, my friends call me, "JJ", or sometimes, "J-two", depending on which bar I'm in. I drive a Peterbilt 18-wheeler for a local freight company in Detroit. Whenever I'm scheduled for a run to Fort Wayne, I like to take Route 12 instead of I-94. Like most truckers, I drink a lot of coffee to stay awake. Along most routes, I know every spot where the food is reasonably good, the toilets are reasonably clean, and parking isn't too difficult. As someone once said, "it goes with the territory". Being road smart is important, and one of the rules is not to pick up any strangers along the way.

Last February, I broke that rule. It was a Tuesday night about 9:00 o'clock. It started to rain when I was just outside Ann Arbor. By the time I passed through Clinton, on Route 12, it was pouring big time! Wipers were slapping back and forth at full speed to keep the windshield clear. I almost didn't see the person walking along side the road. At first I couldn't make out whether it was a man, or a woman. Either way, it was terrible weather to be out in, so I stopped.

"How far you going?" I asked, as my passenger climbed in. He turned out to be a she. I guessed her to be 19 or maybe 20, no older. Her hair appeared to be dark brown and it was plastered to her scalp. As she attempted to wipe some of the rain from her face, I could see freckles.

"Do you know the Route Twelve diner?" I shook my head, I hadn't heard of it. "It's about five or six miles up on the left."

"Sorry I don't know the place, but I'll be happy to drop you off there, if that's where you're going."

"Thanks, I appreciate the lift. Not much traffic out tonight."

"So what brings you out in this rotten weather?" I asked.

"I'm on my way to work. My car isn't running, and a friend was supposed to give me a ride, but he never showed up, so I'm kinda late. I started walking, then it started to rain."

Despite the fact that she was soaked through, she still had a pleasant smile. This young lady didn't appear to let things get to her, like they did me. She had spunk. I tried to remember if I knew of a diner along this stretch of road. I drew a blank. Sometimes when you see something like a sign, you see it so often that you no longer see it when you pass it, but a diner I would certainly remember.

"And you work at this diner?"

"Yep, I'm a waitress there. Got the job my last year in high school. Now, it seems like a long time ago."

"I know what you mean. I've been driving trucks since I got out of school. You got anything else to wear when you get to work? You really did get soaked out there."

"Oh, I'm okay. There are spare uniforms at the diner."

"Good. You got a name?"

"Sure, everybody's got a name."

"Okay, my name's Jay, what's yours?"

"Why?" She seemed cautious, which I understood.

"Just curious, I guess. You don't have to tell me if you don't want to, it's okay."

"Promise you won't laugh if I tell you?"

"I promise."

"It's Juleen. I used to hate it, but now I don't mind it so much. I was born in July, same date as my

Richard Standring

grandmom. Her name's Juleen, too."

"Well if she's Juleen two, that should make you Juleen three." We both laughed at that.

I had never heard the name before, and told her so. She thought it was an old Irish name, but wasn't sure. Since she had been cautious about telling me her name, I decided not to mention that I thought the name went well with her freckles and her easy smile. She might think I was flirting. I wasn't.

"Actually, a daughter from every third generation in my family is named Juleen, and everyone of us has been born in July. It goes back hundreds of years I'm told."

"That's fascinating. Tell me, do they serve good coffee at this diner?"

"Sure do, the best around, and the first cup won't cost you a dime. Service is pretty good, too."

"Sounds great." I started looking to the left of the road. So far, we hadn't passed any lights, or other traffic. That seemed a bit strange. She noticed my concentration on the road. I was looking for the diner.

"You'll see it pretty soon on the left. You can't miss the big green neon sign."

No sooner had she mentioned it, when it appeared. I saw the neon sign, first out of focus, then clear, as the wipers swept through their repeated arc. I put on my turn signal and shifted down. The diner was like a bright beacon against an indigo backdrop. In the parking lot, there were two older cars facing the front entrance. Both were classics. Juleen jumped down from the cab and ran into the diner while I lingered in the rain to admire a beautiful '49 Ford Crestliner tudor. In the light from the diner's windows it appeared to be dark blue. It had oversize fender skirts on the rear, dual chrome exhaust pipes sticking out from under a shiny rear bumper. And there were two chrome spotlights, one on each side of the windshield, both turned down. It was just like the cars my buddies used to drive when I was in high school.

The other car also looked to be in perfect condition. It was a '37 Chevy coupe with a big chrome hood ornament in the shape of a swan and chrome shades sticking out of the headlight rims. The raindrops ran off both cars like they had several coats of wax recently applied.

Somewhere Along the Way

Just seeing those two beauties was worth the stop, and worth getting wet.

Inside, Juleen had a cup of steaming coffee sitting on the counter waiting for me. It was a small diner and very bright inside because everything was either white, or stainless steel. Juleen had changed into a uniform with an apron and didn't look as if she had been outside at all. How did she do that so fast?

She was at the other end of the counter talking to two young guys sitting in a booth by the window. Both had their backs to the window with their legs stretched straight out on the seats. Both wore long side burns, hair combed back into that long ago fashion called a ducktail. And both had on white tee shirts covered with black leather jackets. It looked like the Fonz and his twin brother sitting there. One had a bad case of acne.

In the background, the juke box was playing an old Four Aces song from way back to another time in my life. It was difficult to believe that such a neat place existed here in the middle of nowhere, and I hadn't seen it, or stopped before now. Looking around, I could see the floor and countertops were spotless. If anything was out of place here, it was me. Everything else belonged to the '50s, and I had just taken a step back in time.

The next song was Johnny Ray singing, "Cry". I found myself humming part of it from some distant memory bank. I wanted to ask the two guys in the booth about their cars, but I waited until the piece finished. I wasn't in any hurry to leave. I felt like I was in an episode from "Twighlight Zone".

When the music stopped, I turned and asked, "Those two cars out there are in beautiful shape. Who restored them?"

One turned to the other, "What did he say?" Then one of them looked across the booth at me with a cigarette dangling from his lips like James Dean did years ago in one of his movies. "My chariot is cherry, Dad. With thirty-six hundred miles on it, it don't need restoring, dig?" They both laughed, and Juleen was trying to hide a giggle. Somehow they were sharing a private joke that I didn't quite understand.

"No kidding! Well that Ford is sure a beauty.

32

Richard Standring

Where did you ever find it?"
"Hey, you serious? My old man bought it for me when I finished school last year. 'Course I did a few things to duke it up. Lays rubber pretty good, don't it Bart?" The other guy, with all the acne nodded, all the time grinning.
"Well, I'd sure give just about anything to have one like it. How much do you have in it?" I took a sip of my coffee.
"Oh, maybe eighteen hundred, something like that."
"Uh huh, so what do you figure the car's worth?"
"I just told you, man, eighteen hundred, only it's not for sale, okay? That car is part of my reputation around here, right Bart?"
"You got it, Pete." This time the other one spoke.
It was time for me to leave. I still had a lot of miles ahead of me. Reluctantly I got up. Juleen indicated the coffee was free, so I left her a buck tip. It was worth it just to be in that atmosphere. The two characters in the booth were slightly annoying, yet they, too, fit in with the overall '50s theme of the place. I would definitely stop back. Pulling out of the parking lot, I gave the horn a few blasts and listened to the steady clack, clack beat of the wipers once again. Fog was starting to develop, so I kept my attention on the road, while humming a few old pieces almost forgotten. I thought about my senior prom and all the great songs that were popular then. They all came back to me. South Bend arrived quickly.

Two weeks later I had another opportunity to take Route 12. I was looking forward to hearing a few golden oldies and having a bite to eat at my newly discovered mystery diner. I had mentioned it to a few other drivers but no one seemed to know about it. That made it all the more special. I had scheduled this trip so that I'd be there before dark, however I was late pulling out of the terminal.
Once again, it was dark. But this time, it was a clear night. I'd probably see that green neon sign a mile before I got there. As I neared the spot where I

Somewhere Along the Way

estimated Juleen had been when I picked her up, I began to get excited and started humming some old songs from the past. Five minutes went by and I still hadn't seen any signs of the diner. Seven minutes, I slowed down to 35 and let a few cars pass me. I had to be close. Five more minutes passed, still nothing. How could I have missed it? The road was dark on both sides for miles. Without a convenient place to turn around, I had to continue. A sour taste came to my mouth and I reached into my jacket for a mint. How could I have missed it?

It was another two weeks before I had a chance to try Route 12 again. This time, I was traveling the other way, back to Ann Arbor. And, this time I made sure I would pass through the entire area in daylight. No way would I miss the diner this time. But I did!

Exasperated, I pulled into a nearby gas station and asked the young attendant if he knew where the Route 12 diner was?

"Ain't no diner around here, Mister. Hasn't been for years." He could read my disappointment. "You sure you got the right highway?" I nodded that I did, but I was beginning to wonder if maybe it was all a dream. After all, wouldn't some of the other truckers know about such a neat place?

"Tell you what, just wait here a minute. I'll call my aunt. She knows everything there is to know about these parts better'n anyone. Maybe she can help." With that he picked up the phone. He seemed eager to help, that surprised me.

"I appreciate that," was all I could say. The diner haunted my thoughts. I'd told my wife about the old cars in the parking lot, and my hope that perhaps sometime one of them might be for sale. If so, I wanted to have a sufficient balance in my checkbook. If Pete showed up in his '49 Ford, I was prepared to offer him four thousand dollars for it... for openers. I'd probably go as high as six knowing it was worth at least twice that, if not more.

When I'm nervous, I chew gum. I took out a stick while waiting for the gas station attendant to reach his aunt on the phone. What I heard raised goose bumps on my arms.

"Hello, Aunt Juleen? It's Henry down at the pumps.

There's a trucker here askin' about a diner supposed to be 'round here. He seems to think it's close by...."

After a long minute, the shock wore off and I asked, "Can I speak with your aunt?" It was the second time I'd ever heard the name Juleen, and that had to be more than a coincidence. I was beginning to wonder if my mind was playing tricks on me until this very minute.

"Sorry, she hung up. She said to tell you that the diner you're lookin' for is about four miles back that way." He pointed down the road, the way I had just come. "She said some trucker always asks about that diner every five years. Must have something to do with leap year."

"Thanks. Tell me something, Henry. Is your aunt Juleen a young woman? Maybe in her early twenties?"

"No sir, she's old. I guess she's in her seventies. Why?"

"Oh, just curious. Juleen is such an unusual name. It's Irish, isn't it?"

"Yep. And yer in the Irish Hills right now."

As I crawled up into the cab, I had the distinct feeling that something was wrong. I was determined to find that diner. I was sure it was on Route 12, and I couldn't believe that I would miss it two different times in the past month, particularly when I was looking for it. I was driving slowly with my flashers on, so other vehicles would know to pass. Suddenly there it was!

Only what I saw, were the remnants of a diner sitting back from the road half hidden by tall weeds. Rust covered much of the outside. All the windows were gone. A few broken pieces of glass reflected the late afternoon light. It was a sad sight to behold, and I was disappointed. This was the very same diner, in exactly the same place, only the parking area had disappeared into tall weeds. And the neon sign was gone. No wonder I hadn't noticed it before. I was watching for a bright green neon sign. Somehow the diner seemed much smaller than I remembered. At least it did exist, but somehow a period of many years came and went during the past few weeks.

I was definitely looking at a ghost from the past; a ghost diner that only came back to life every five years,

Somewhere Along the Way

on leap year. I'd have to wait another five years to see Juleen and have another cup of coffee there.

Meanwhile, it was a story too bizarre to mention to anyone without sounding like a candidate for the funny farm. Five years is a long time to wait for another special cup of coffee, but I'm looking forward to it. I'll be there, just wait and see. Hopefully Juleen will be there, too.

End

Author's note: While this is fiction, Route 12 does exist in Michigan. It passes through an area known as Irish Hills, where the rusted remains of a '50s diner was once seen along this stretch of road. The author has a photo as proof. Everything else is just the kind of tale an Irishman might tell on St. Patrick's Day, on leap year.

Richard Standring

Remnants

Just an old windsock,
Tattered and torn,
Still seeking out a breeze.

Just an old hangar door,
Battered and worn,
Still squeaking a rusty refrain.

Just an old pasture now,
With weeds grown tall.
Here, gallant men once flew.

That old windsock, and,
That old hangar door,
Remnants of an airfield I knew.

RAS

In memory of Mather Airport on Ridge Rd. in Brooklyn, Ohio where Edgar & Arlo taught many to fly.

Somewhere Along the Way

Richard Standring

INCIDENT AT HILLSIDE ELEMENTARY

Alan Peters was en route to another assignment when his editor paged him and told him to cover the Hillside Elementary School incident. Apparently an old biplane had crash-landed in the playground area.

Having been with the newspaper for only six months, Alan was eager for any assignment that would get him on the front page. His mentor had told him numerous times, regardless of the assignment, small details made human interest stories more worthwhile reading. "Don't forget the small details," Alan recited several times, like a mantra, to himself while driving to the crash site.

"I understand you actually saw the accident, is that correct?" Alan asked the old man standing near the wreckage. Alan was asking questions while at the same time, taking pictures with his digital camera.

"Yep, saw the whole thing. Looked to me like he was trying to land that antique biplane and just didn't have enough room. Almost made it." Mr. Gentry was wearing faded bib overalls, a plaid flannel shirt and straw hat, proof enough he was a farmer. The old gentleman indicated he lived nearby, pointing to a house across the road.

"Who called the ambulance?" Alan asked.

"I did, of course. Saw the pilot crawl out of the rear cockpit and fall to the ground. I ran over and helped him stand up. He kept shaking his head and asking me where the airfield was. I ran across the road there and used Mrs. Caraway's phone to call EMS. They got here pretty quick."

"Where did the emergency crew take him?"

Somewhere Along the Way

"Shucks, I don't know. The hospital I would imagine."

"Yes, but which one? I'd like to interview the pilot."

"Well I guess you'll just have to check with the EMS folks who picked him up. Didn't appear to be bleeding. He was wearing an old leather jacket. Had one of those silk scarves wrapped around his neck, like they used to wear in the old days, along with a helmet and goggles. Reminded me of the days when they flew planes just like that one over there."

"Uh huh," Alan had about as much information as he was going to get, and was about to leave so he could check with the EMS people on where they took the pilot.

"Like I said, they used to fly those things out of here years ago... when I was a youngster."

"Pardon me, did you say fly out of *here*? Where did they fly from *exactly*?" Alan sensed there may be an interesting twist here. *Remember the small details*, he reminded himself.

"Right where we're standing. Years ago, before you were born, and before this here school was built, this was once an airfield. They flew biplanes just like that one. On Sunday, you could take a ride for fifty cents."

"So this used to be an airport... before the school was built?"

"That's what I just said. But it was a long time ago. Before the school was here, it was a farm for a long time. Land belonged to a family named... let me see if I can remember. Nope, but it will come to me."

"That's okay, I'll check back with you later. Maybe you'll recall it when you've had some time." Alan scribbled Mr. Gentry's phone number on his notepad. A crowd had gathered around the plane. A deputy was motioning for everyone to stay back. Alan had a deadline to make. He was thinking that maybe there would be an interesting follow-up story.

"Excuse me, can you tell me where you took the pilot from the plane crash at Hillside School?" Alan asked the EMS dispatcher.

"I'm sorry, we didn't handle that call."
Alan's annoyance grew with each phone call and visit he made. Nobody would acknowledge picking up an injured pilot. And, none of the medical clinics, or nearby hospitals, had admitted such a patient in the last 24 hours. It was becoming a puzzle.

The pictures of the wrecked biplane turned out well. The old aircraft had flipped over, smashing the wooden propeller and the vertical tail section. One wheel strut had collapsed while the other remaining wheel pointed upward toward the sky. The fabric wings were crumpled with wires and struts sticking out. Alan had to turn the print upside down to read the markings on the tail section. It showed, NC 1099J.

A pilot friend told Alan that the biplane appeared to be a Curtiss JN4D Jenny, a popular trainer in the '20s, right after World War I.

Not being able to locate the pilot for an interview, Alan exhausted his frustration at the library going through books on old aircraft. He found additional information about the Jenny and learned that it had a water-cooled OX-5 engine and it could fly about 80 miles per hour. His next stop was the newspaper archives.

In no time, Alan had an intense headache from scrolling through reel after reel of microfiche film covering the past 10 years. Later he found an article on the Hillside Elementary School being built in 1954. No mention of the land having been an airport previously.

He continued his search after taking a coffee break. Finally, on a reel covering May, 1933, he found a picture of the aircraft. It was the very same biplane with the same markings on the vertical tail section.

The man standing next to the plane was identified as E.J. Calverly. Alan was fascinated with what he discovered next. Just as Mr. Gentry had indicated, this picture was taken at the Brooklyn Aerodrome on Ridge Road, the same location as the recent accident.

The next reel revealed something more interesting:

Local Pilot and Aircraft Missing

Somewhere Along the Way

CLEVELAND OH -- On April 18th 1934, pilot E.J. Calverly took off from the Brooklyn Aerodrome on Ridge Rd. He was flying a Jenny biplane he recently purchased. Those at the airfield who knew him, said Mr. Calverly was an excellent pilot, yet he and his aircraft remain missing. No crashes have been reported in the immediate and surrounding area. The aircraft has a maximum range of approximately 300 miles. A search of the entire maximum range area, including Lake Erie, has been conducted. While there is some mystery surrounding this recent disappearance, it is presumed the aircraft crashed into the lake. Mr. Calverly's destination is unknown. His family was not aware of any plans for a long trip. The disappearance remains a mystery.

Alan read the article several times before everything began to sink in. He had a story, but he wouldn't be able to write it, because nobody, including his editor, would believe it. The pilot, and this biplane, had been missing for over 60 years... and had just returned! Alan didn't believe the incident was a hoax, or some public relations stunt. It was something that could easily have appeared as an episode on "Twilight Zone".

His story about the plane crash appeared, but the follow-up story, about the missing pilot and the plane returning after 60 years, was scratched. Alan suffered a few snickers back at the editorial office.

That story remained untold... until now.

End

Richard Standring

The Dixie

Highway 133 is a four-lane divided road that runs north and south, connecting Mount Union and Valley Junction, 18 miles to the south. With a 70-mile per hour speed limit, most motorists don't notice or appreciate the passing landscape on either side of the highway.
One interesting, and easily missed, item is an old dilapidated drive-in theatre beside a parallel two-lane road that was once known as the Dixie Highway before Route 133 materialized, changing the adjacent scene forever.
The Dixie drive-in was once a popular spot, drawing crowds from both towns. It closed in 1972, about the sane tune that Route 133 was being built. To build Highway 133, many old farms became divided and ancient tobacco barns disappeared to make way for the progress. The landscape slowly changed and with it The Dixie continued on its downward spiral to decay. Several abandoned motels on the two-lane road experienced a similar fate. The Dixie is uniquely positioned halfway between the two small southern towns and currently provides space and questionable shelter for Saturday flea market activity.
Most of the big screen remains standing on a precarious support structure that appears ready to collapse. The rusting marquis at the entrance steal bears **The Dixie** in faded letters. The neon tubing and light bulbs have been broken for 30 years. The structure seems to be losing its battle to survive yet it remains as a fleeting reminder of another era. Gone are all the pipe stands and speakers in the parking lot.
It was Saturday afternoon, when for some strange reason, Ricky Jenkins decided to stop by the flea market and browse for an unknown bargain. He parked his truck in the center area of the old drive-in, not far from the central concrete block building that once served as

Somewhere Along the Way

the projection booth and refreshment stand. He spent an hour absent-mindedly going from one vendor to another, not seeing anything of real interest.

Periodically he would look up at the decaying curved screen with missing panels that provided a backdrop to the flea market activity. Ricky recalled his parents talking about their courtship days and evenings spent watching double features at The Dixie in the early '50s. His father owned a 1950 DeSoto Convertible then. Ricky still had a picture of it somewhere.

Bored, Ricky felt an impulse to investigate what used to be the refreshment stand. The windows were caked with years of dust and dirt. He had to scrape away a layer to peek inside. He could just make out what must have been the serving counter. On a far wall he saw a faded poster advertising an upcoming feature. He strained to focus on the details, cupping his hands to his temples and pressing against the dirty glass to see inside the darkened room.

Suddenly the room became illuminated. It was as if a light switch had been turned on. A young man wearing a white apron was standing behind the counter beckoning Ricky to come inside. The padlocked door was now open. Once inside the aroma of fresh popcorn surrounded him.

"What can I get you? Better hurry, the movie is about to start," the young man said. He had a friendly smile and looked directly at Ricky.

"I seem to be the only one here," Ricky replied. The young man handed him a box of warm buttered popcorn.

"Oh don't worry, they'll arrive eventually. Right now, you're our only customer."

Ricky examined the poster on the wall. In the bright light he could see the title clearly, "Rebel without a Cause" starring James Dean, Natalie Wood and Dennis Hopper. Another poster featured "Picnic" with William Holden and Kim Novak. Turning around, Ricky discovered it was now dark outside. He had no trouble finding his parked truck. It was right where he had parked it earlier, except now there was a pipe stand beside it and a speaker box was hanging on the driver's side window. Ricky decided he had to be dreaming all this. He opened the truck door, got in and settled back to watch the beginning of the movie now on the big curved, unblemished screen before him. It was better than any big-screen TV he'd ever seen.

An instant later, there was a tap on the side window. A deputy sheriff was standing beside Ricky's truck, motioning for him to lower the window. The speaker had vanished.
"Sir, I'll have to ask you to leave. The flea market is closed."
"What?" Ricky was confused. The screen was now dark and he could see the missing panels. The lights were out in the refreshment stand. Had he been imagining all this? It had seemed so real. Or had he simply been dreaming?
"Sir, are you okay to drive?" The officer asked.
"Yes. Yes, I'm fine. I must have dozed off. Sorry."
On the way home, Ricky was still haunted by the experience at the flea market and drive-in theatre. Somehow by thinking about another time, he had drifted into a dreamlike state, and for a brief moment, had traveled back for a quick glimpse of what The Dixie had been like in 1955, when his parents were dating. It was almost as if he'd really been there. The posters were still vivid in his mind. Nobody would ever believe his recent bizarre experience, he thought to himself, so it would be best not to ever mention it to anyone.
As he got out of the truck, Ricky spotted an empty popcorn box with a few remaining kernels on the floor. It was at that precise moment Ricky realized he had a mission to accomplish. Somehow, he would find a way to buy the old drive-in theatre and restore it to its former condition. The flea market gypsies would have to move somewhere else.
Ricky decided he would feature old classic movies with stars like John Wayne, Rock Hudson, Peter Sellers and Doris Day. And, he'd be sure to serve hot buttered popcorn. Anyone arriving in a classic automobile, prior to 1970, would get in at half-price. Eventually the crowd

Somewhere Along the Way

would come, just as the young man behind the counter had promised. Ricky was convinced The Dixie had chosen him for the job. It would be his special project for the next few years, restoring the drive-in to its past while re-introducing some classic movies.

End

Richard Standring

Rattlesnake Bend

At Rattlesnake Bend, you can't make a friend,
    You're better off not trying.
    Folks out there, just don't seem to care,
    If you're alive, or dying.

At Rattlesnake Bend, you'd best not stay,
    Even for a little while.
    Folks out there, just stand and stare,
    No "hello," never a smile.

At Rattlesnake Bend, some call it the end,
    It's a desolate place to be.
    If you've ever been there, just keep it,
    A secret between you and me.

Rattlesnake Bend, disappeared with the wind,
    Gone now without a trace.
    Never again, will anyone spend,
    Time in that terrible place.

                                RAS

Somewhere Along the Way

Richard Standring

Corporate Doublespeak and Other Lies

Most companies in trouble today, didn't arrive at that critical point suddenly. They gravitated to that destination over a period of time, complacent that things were going well, or as planned. Top management didn't recognize the danger signals along the way.

Or, key executives had a hidden agenda and knew very well what the company's position was and where it was headed. Survival deals and golden parachutes are being lined up and company stock is being quietly sold.

Sometimes it takes an outside force/event to get the company's attention, to focus on the critical areas. Mergers, acquisitions, and potential strategic alliances uncover the undesirable aspects the company has ignored, or hasn't recognized, as a significant problem. It's when the deal falls through, that anyone hears the wake up call. Soon after the failed merger attempt, a scapegoat is usually sacrificed to appease the stockholders. Sometimes it's an early retirement announcement. A new CFO may be introduced, and damage control goes into motion.

If the stock is publicly traded, a price drop is inevitable. This is usually followed by another announcement that the company is reorganizing.

Here's an example of what can happen: For years, a major lending company (in the sub-prime mortgage market) was running creative, attention-getting television commercials. They had offices throughout the U.S. At one point their stock was trading at $36 per share. They started looking for another financial partner, for a possible merger or acquisition arrangement, so they could expand their services and have access to more capital. A major search firm was

Somewhere Along the Way

hired to handle the flirtation process.

Meanwhile, the stock declined to $16 per share. Insiders scrambled to buy what they could, knowing that once a larger bank was tagged as a partner, the stock would no doubt soar.

But it didn't happen. A series of large financial institutions looked at the company closely, then one after another declined the offer to merge. They dis-covered an overlooked problem area, and backed away. After numerous turn downs, the company began a realignment program. Poor performing branch offices were closed. Expenses were closely monitored, and company vehicles were eliminated.

Soon, the stock dropped to less than one dollar per share! Eventually, they had to bite the old bullet and file chapter eleven. A lot of money was lost, as well as jobs! Competitors took full advantage of the situation. Few on the inside believed that it could ever happen. I was one of many who lost a sizeable investment with that company. I quit just prior to their filing for bankruptcy.

The Chopping Block Blues is a sad tune to play, to loyal employees who have believed, and followed, the party line. These team players are a valuable resource. They are shocked when the pink slips are distributed. It's a grim realization, and too late for finger pointing. Layoffs are part of the sacrificial ceremony, rationalized as necessary *"To adjust the bottom line"*.

Phrases like: *"We're re-evaluating the marketplace and the potential"* really means... "We stubbed our toe, and we need to rethink our position. Is the future worth pursuing?" Another gem is: *"Everyone needs to stay focused, and be assured that we continue to be a major player."* Translation... "We're trying to buy some time to figure out what we want to do." And, *"We're exploring all our options"* can be construed as... "We're holding out for the best offer". When two corporations are merging, they frequently announce, *"Everyone's job is secure, no changes are anticipated."* That's when it's time to update the resume and start looking around.

Listen carefully to what isn't being said. When a company is in deep trouble, there can be no guarantees for anyone. The company must do whatever is necessary to survive. Memos, about watching expenses, can be an early alert, particularly if everyone has been mindful of expenses all along. When the company cars are eliminated, and all travel plans are put on hold, you know there's a serious financial problem. You don't need a big auditing firm to translate that for you.

At the same time, a few good, talented people will leave... and the company will never be the same again. That's the sad reality of getting bigger, expanding into new markets, then realizing too late that the move was a big mistake. There are few winners. Everyone else must endure some pain without any gain, unless you get lucky and land another, better position. That sometimes happens to those who recognize the early warning signs. For everyone else... *"It's business as usual, nothing to worry about"*. Yeah, right!

The Enron Scandal is another example of what can happen when the empire starts to crumble. The sad facts are that there were people (high up on the food chain) who knew the truth and benefited from the cover-ups. Even some well-known accounting firms eventually got caught, and fined, for looking the other way. Even while the danger signals were blaring, stock brokers were still touting the company's stock as a good buy. The lies trickled all the way down the line.

So who can you trust in troubled times? Trust your instincts if you work for the company. Keep your eyes and ears open and read between the lines on all those memos mentioned earlier. If you have a friend in the Accounts Payable Dept. you might inquire if the company is staying current on the incoming invoices? If they're running 120 days late, and they're getting reminders and threatening calls from suppliers, or the company is placed on a C.O.D. basis, you have reason to be concerned. There's a cash flow problem.

Larger corporations have a board of directors whose mission is to monitor the Chairman, CEO, CFO and President, and make recommendations. Interestingly enough, most board members are selected by the Chairman or CEO. Yes, stockholders get to vote on the election of board members, but that rarely has any

Somewhere Along the Way

significant influence, since top management holds proxies for millions of shares. It begs the question, who is watching the board of directors and making sure they do their job?

Those who know the answer, charge big bucks for their financial advice, so the little guy has a difficult time knowing when trouble is brewing early enough to get out safely, or avoid the trap. Perhaps in time, savings accounts will re-emerge as a suitable, safe alternative to other forms of investments.

End

Richard Standring

Bad Day at Flat Rock

    Dying wasn't something Tyler Cantrell thought much about. Yet before the day would end, he'd be thinking about it a lot.
    Most days, Tyler liked his job, inspecting mobile homes for the bank, prior to being repossessed. He'd take pictures inside and out and write a descriptive condition report, noting if the appliances were missing, and any damage. His biggest problem was locating the homes, because some were in remote areas where the roads didn't have signs, and mailboxes didn't have numbers. Frequently he had to stop and ask for directions. When he did that, he always wore a baseball-type cap and bought a soft drink. He found people were much more cooperative when he became a customer and looked friendly.
    Flat Rock was one of those remote places, hidden away in the foothills of the Smoky Mountains. The single-wide mobile home he was looking for was down an unmarked gravel road, about two miles off the highway. The driveway to the site was considerably worse. It was uphill, and appeared to be just a washed-out, rutted clearing that could hardly be called anything more than a path. Getting the home out was definitely going to be a problem; somebody's else's problem. Never the less, Tyler took a picture from the road, looking up at the home in the distance, to give someone an idea of the challenge they were faced with. He left his car at the base of the so-called drive and proceeded to climb the steep hill, being careful where he stepped. It had recently rained and there was a lot of mud, making it easy to slip and fall.
    After taking several pictures outside the mobile home, Tyler walked to the back door. It was closer to the ground than the front door, where the deck had been removed, making it impossible for anyone to enter. His

master keys worked about 90 per cent of the time. The other 10 per cent required the use of a few special tools. Back doors rarely had dead bolt locks, making the entry process much easier.

Concrete blocks were stacked three tiers high to form a makeshift set of steps to the back door. The last step was still two feet from the threshold. Being 63 years old, Tyler preferred not having to climb into raised doorways without steps. He was getting too old for gymnastics, something his wife frequently mentioned. His master key worked. As he opened the door, he was aware of how quiet it was. The house sat on the side of a hill and backed up to a dense wooded area. For just a slight moment, Tyler felt apprehensive as he pushed open the door. He was expecting to be hit with the stench of rotten food and garbage, and was surprised. The odor he smelled was much different. At first he couldn't identify it. When he entered the kitchen, the smell was stronger and he quickly realized the source. The kitchen was a meth lab! Jars of various ingredients were sitting on the counter.

A portable propane camping stove, with a pan sitting on it, contained a cement-like mixture dried inside. It reminded him of day-old oatmeal only it smelled terrible. Tyler took several pictures of the kitchen laboratory before taking a brief tour. Two bedrooms had large holes kicked in the walls and there were stains on the carpet. He found an old washer and dryer in the laundry area and looked inside the dryer, out of curiosity.

To his surprise, he found a clear plastic bag, similar to what dry cleaners use to cover garments. The bag was full of marijuana leaves. Tyler lifted the lid on the washer and found a dozen large zip-lock bags stuffed with money. He reached inside and withdrew all the bags. He searched the kitchen and found an unused garbage bag and stuffed the zip-lock bags into it, walked to the open back door and threw the bag to the ground. He had no idea how much money was there. He'd count it later.

Tyler knew this was a dangerous situation he'd stumbled upon. He'd notify the sheriff's office when he got back into town. He'd left his cell phone in the car because it was useless in this area. He couldn't get a signal, so he didn't bother to carry it. Never the less, he made a mental note to keep it with him on future inspections, in case an emergency occurred. That flashing thought added to his current apprehension.

Stepping out the door, onto the first concrete step, took some careful coordination. He was concentrating on making a silent departure when the cinderblock step suddenly moved, breaking into several pieces. Tyler's momentum continued forward sending him sprawling into the weeds. He felt a jab of pain in his left ankle as it twisted. He was kneeling on the ground, still holding the digital camera, when he heard sounds of two approaching vehicles. He listened carefully and determined it was two all-terrain four-wheelers, and they were getting closer! Normally he would be grateful for help, but considering the situation, he decided it was probably better to remain hidden in the tall grass and weeds. He grabbed the garbage bag and crawled into the high grass hiding behind some bushes.

There was no way he could reach his car before the two riders arrived. He knew his sprained ankle wouldn't support him enough for him to run. On his hands and knees, he crawled into the tall brush hoping to hide in the wooded area beyond. He could hear voices once they shut off their engines. Two young men were beside his car, checking it out.

"Hey, Odell. Whoever is snooping around here left his cell phone on the seat of the car. And lookee here, he also left the keys in the ignition. Hee, hee."

"Well he's blocking the drive. Guess we oughta move it out of the way, what d'ya think?"

"Good idea. Maybe we should park it in the pond over yonder."

"Yeah, let's do that."

Tyler watched from his hiding spot among the tall weeds. On impulse, Tyler turned on the digital camera, put it on the zoom mode and took a picture of the two men at the end of the drive. One of them started his car and backed it onto the gravel road. Tyler silently uttered a curse for leaving the keys and his cell phone in the car.

Somewhere Along the Way

Now they were taking his car, leaving one ATV behind. He doubted he could reach it, not being able to walk. He had no idea when they would return. Instinct told him he had to escape before things became worse. If only his ankle would cooperate, he could move into the woods and hope to find his way back to the highway, keeping out of sight until he got there.

 He crawled into what looked like an overgrown cornfield. The stalks were turning brown. A few rows into the crop, Tyler came upon several tall leafy plants. He recognized the marijuana instantly. It certainly wasn't a safe place to hide. Once again he attempted to stand forcing himself to endure the pain from his throbbing ankle. He hobbled towards the woods and farther away from the field and the mobile home. Eventually they'd come looking for him and they had the advantage of fast mobility, as well as knowing the terrain. Tyler had no idea where the nearest farm house might be.

 A few minutes later, the noise from the two ATVs reverberated in the woods. They sounded close. Tyler could also feel his heart beating and knew he was on the verge of a panic attack. Trying to remain calm and hidden was his primary objective. He thought back to his days in the Army when he trained to evade capture by the enemy. That was a lifetime ago, but some things were just common sense. It was late afternoon and he was able to determine which way was West. The highway was in the opposite direction. Two miles, moving at a snail's pace through dense woods would seem more like twenty miles. And by then it would be totally dark. It would be doubly difficult not to make any noise and give away his position. Just the snapping of a dead branch would be amplified.

 While in the woods, Tyler slipped several times causing additional pressure to his ankle. He had to grit his teeth to keep from yelling out in pain. Fearing he might accidentally lose the camera, Tyler ejected the disc putting it in his jacket pocket. He put the camera into the garbage bag with the money and tied it to a low hanging branch. He'd retrieve it later. He didn't want to be caught with the money or the camera. He continued to move through the woods, going from tree to tree for support. He could hear the two ATVs roaring around on the hillside like two angry wasps. Fortunately, the woods was too dense for the vehicles to operate. Tyler thought about a movie he'd seen a long time ago about four stranded men attempting to canoe down a remote river in northern Georgia. He felt he was in a similar predicament.

After what seemed like an hour, Tyler crested the ridge and looking down, spotted another smaller mobile home. There was an old Ford pickup truck parked in the yard. Sliding, hobbling and crawling, he slowly worked his way down the hillside, making sure to remain in tall grass for cover. He hated snakes and thought about what he'd do if he stumbled upon one. Probably die of a heart attack, he thought. He immediately forced that thought from his mind. He had to think positive. All the while his sore ankle continued to swell.

When he got to within 50 yards of the mobile home, Tyler waited and watched for any sign of someone inside. He didn't hear, or see anything. Slowly he approached the pickup truck and noticed a flatbed trailer hooked to the rear. Opening the driver's side door with great care, so as not to make any noise, was a futile effort. It was an old truck and the door gave a protesting squeak. He had hoped to find keys in the ignition, but there weren't any. He'd have to try hot-wiring it and hope there was enough gas to get him back to the small town of Flat Rock where he'd get help.

He was leaning under the dash when a voice startled him.

"Just what the hell d'ya think yer doin'?" It was a young woman and she was pointing a pistol directly at him from the doorway.

"I didn't know anyone was here. I need your help. Do you have a phone I can use?"

"You must be the dude Dennis and Odell are lookin' for. They said someone was up here snoopin' around," she said.

"Please. I wasn't snooping. I work for the bank and I was up here checking on that mobile home on the other side of the ridge when your two friends arrived. They

Somewhere Along the Way

took my car. That's stealing by the way." He thought about the irony of his remark, the garbage bag full of money still in the woods. Wasn't that stealing?

"Oh yeah? Ask me if I care. When them two get back, you won't be around long to cause any more trouble. Get in here where I can keep an eye on you."

Tyler hobbled up the steps to the deck and through the open door. It was sparse inside. There was a table with two chairs and a mattress on the living room floor. A portable disc player was beside the mattress. While watching the house, Tyler saw the power pole beside the house without a meter. So there was no electricity. He didn't see a portable phone.

"Wasn't exactly expecting company, so I didn't bother to clean, not that it matters any. Sit wherever you want, just don't do anything sudden-like."

"How long have the three of you lived out here?" Tyler asked hoping to get the young woman to talk. He estimated her age to be around 19 or 20.

"We move around a lot. We been here just long enough for me to get pregnant, don't that beat all."

"So which one of the two is the father?"

"What's it to you? Besides, I'm not exactly for sure."

"So is this Odell your boyfriend?"

"Nah, he's just someone Dennis and I hooked up with. He's one mean dude. You're gonna find that out real soon."

"He the one who owns this land?"

"You sure ask a lot of questions. Nah, he don't own nothing' but that there truck outside. Old man who owned this place died. It was kinda sudden. I think they buried him somewhere out back. Problee plant you out there, too."

This just confirmed his earlier fears. He was in deep trouble and this young lady wasn't about to help him. Yet his best chance to escape was before the two men returned. The longer he waited, the less chance he had. After a few minutes, Tyler said he had to use the toilet and wondered if there was any running water.

"Okay, but leave the door open. You can't get out the window no how. And use that bucket with the water in it to flush the commode. You have to pour some into the tank, then push down the handle."

He used the toilet, leaving the door ajar. He saw the plastic pail and used part of the water to flush the commode. He waited holding the bucket, letting the door block her view.

"Hey, you done in there? Come on out. And don't try anything funny, I got this gun pointed at you."

Tyler continued to wait, not saying anything. Soon she pushed open the door. When it opened, he threw the half full pail of water in her face and lunged forward knocking her to the floor. The pistol flew out of her hand. He hated to hit her, but he did, more as a reaction. She was out cold. Tyler crawled over her to get the gun. He checked and found it loaded.

He found an old dirty sheet and tore a few strips to bind her arms to her side and tie her ankles together. He stuffed a piece in her mouth as well. Then he tore another strip and bound his ankle as tightly as he could manage. A quick search of the kitchen didn't produce any truck keys. In a closet, he found a 12-guage shotgun along with a box of shells. The shotgun was also loaded. He wondered if the two young men on the ATVs were armed?

Hobbling toward the door, the young woman started pounding her bound feet against the floor. Tyler removed the gag long enough to ask a question.

"Where is the key to the truck?"

"Take me with you and I'll I tell you. Otherwise, you'll have to walk and they'll catch you for sure."

"Why do you want to leave?"

"Odell finds me here and his truck gone, he'll beat me real good. It's time I got away from those two. Untie me and I'll get the key."

"Okay, but try anything, like screaming, and I'll clock you again only harder next time."

Tyler pointed the pistol at her following her out the door. He had the shotgun in his left hand the pistol in his right. "You drive," he said. The idea of depressing a clutch pedal with his sprained left ankle didn't appeal to him.

She unhooked the trailer, started the truck, popped

the clutch and spun the rear wheels, spraying the deck with stones and dirt. "We're outta here!" she yelled.

The truck was old, but it had a powerful engine that roared. His pursuers would hear them now and come racing after them. The noise from the truck's dual mufflers blocked out the noise of the approaching ATVs behind them. Tyler saw them coming in the cracked side mirror. The young woman saw them, too and floored the gas pedal. She turned the wheel left then right producing a cloud of dust behind them.

Suddenly the two ATVs were on each side of them. Tyler stuck the shotgun out the open window and pulled the trigger without aiming. He hit the front of the ATV and saw it flip in the air. Tyler pumped another shell into the breach and leaned across the seat. The other ATV fell back behind them and continued to follow them all the way to the hard surfaced highway. The woman didn't stop when they tuned onto the highway. Tyler held his breath hoping there was no approaching traffic.

"So where are we going?" the young woman asked. She seemed unconcerned about the last few dramatic minutes. Young people had that quality.

"We're going to find the sheriff, or a deputy, and tell them what happened."

"Are they going to arrest me and put me in jail?" Suddenly she sounded like a scared little girl.

"I don't know. What's your name?"

"Cassie. My real name is Theresa, but everyone calls me Cassie."

"Tell me something, Cassie. When you were pointing this gun at me back there in the trailer, would you have shot me?"

"I ain't never shot anyone before, so I don't know. Odell is the one who's done all the killin'. That's why I decided to leave, before he killed me, too. When he gets buzzed, he does some really weird stuff. I don't think he was too happy to hear I was knocked up."

"Where are you from?"

"A place you never heard of in Arkansas. My grandpaw has a farm back there. I been thinking' of goin' back sometime after the baby is born."

"You need to go back before that. Grandparents

always love their grandkids, regardless of where you've been, or what you've done. You need to go back and make some new friends. Stop hanging around with druggies like Dennis and Odell. People like that will get you killed."

"Tell me about it. I thought about trying to run once, but I knew they'd find me and then there'd be all kinds of hell to pay. When I saw you were gonna leave me there, and take Odell's truck, I knew it was time to scoot. Probably my last chance."

They were approaching the small town of Flat Rock. Tyler was searching for any type of law enforcement vehicle he could find. They hadn't been followed. That's when Tyler saw a Hardee's fast food restaurant.

"Pull over there and stop." Tyler reached for his wallet and pulled out a five dollar bill. He handed the money to Cassie. It left him with just ten dollars, but he had that stash back in the woods waiting to be retrieved later. He still had no idea how much money was in the garbage bag. "Here. Take this money, buy something to eat and take your time. I'll be back shortly and drop you off in Johnson City. Then you can catch a bus back home. I suggest you don't talk to anyone, either."

"You're letting me go? Why? I almost shot you."

"Yeah, but it didn't happen, so you're getting another chance. Take it before I change my mind. Do you think you can kill some time in there?"

"Mister, I've been killin' time for the last year. Yeah, I think I can handle that."

Tyler spent a half hour with the sheriff explaining what happened. He turned over the disc from his camera as evidence. He never mentioned Cassie and hoped she took his advice. He was still debating about whether or not to mention the money he'd found. After all, he'd lost his car, ruined his clothes and twisted an ankle. And, there was all the trauma and aggravation to consider. Surely there was a price for being exposed to danger. This was Tyler's rationalization for not talking about the trash bag still hidden in the woods.

Somewhere Along the Way

Tyler had to admit, it was a bizarre story. While he was relating the events, the sheriff dispatched two deputies to check out the area Tyler had just left. A few minutes later, one called in to report that a mobile home was on fire along with a cornfield and the woods behind the home. The volunteer fire department was notified. Being in such a remote area, it was unlikely that anything could be saved. The deputies didn't find any ATVs or Tyler's Chevy four-door.

Drinking a cup of bad coffee in the sheriff's office, Tyler decided that greed sure had a way of biting you in the buns. Maybe it was time to retire. This last mobile home inspection was a little too exciting, and too strenuous to suit him. Suddenly he felt his age.

Tyler was glad he never counted the money in the trash bag. Now he'd never know how much he'd lost. It could have been worse, he conceded, he could have been killed.

End

Richard Standring

River Dreaming

There's a river in his dreams,
    Flowing slowly,
    Always moving.

Bending shoreline, so it seems,
    Many harbors,
    Always waiting.

Coal barges head to Orleans,
    Tugboats pushing,
    Always working.

Paddle wheelers, call them Queens,
    Toot their passing,
    Always splashing.

Take a ride, if you have means,
    Maybe someday,
    Always dreaming.

            RAS

Somewhere Along the Way

Richard Standring

Gigolo Sunset

 A friend recommended Georgio's whenever I was in Miami, and looking for an excellent Italian meal. He said they also served the best drinks in town. And, if the bartender had to rely on any notes, or cards, to make a drink, it was on the house. For me, a gin & tonic isn't that difficult to make, and since I was in the area, I decided to check out this highly-touted restaurant.
 At 7:30, the dining room was completely full, confirming the popularity of the place. I sat at the bar surveying the scene, I wasn't in any hurry to eat. Sitting a few seats away, I couldn't help notice an attractive lady. She appeared to be in her mid to late 50s. She was wearing a simple white shift that stopped just above her knees. Her pearl necklace looked equally expensive. *Elegant* was the only word I could think of to describe her. Her blond hair was cut short and styled. She reminded me of a movie actress who's name escaped me. I tried not to stare at her. She was sitting alone. That surprised me. However, the bartender seemed to know her.
 I was on my second gin & tonic, and she was on her third martini. At least I think it was her third, when she smiled my way and lifted her glass in a salute.
 "Here's to beautiful sunsets", she said in a deep sexy voice. Then she patted the empty seat next to her, motioning for me to join her. "Are you waiting for someone?" she asked.
 "No, just the beautiful sunset." It was all I could think of to say. It sounded corny.
 "In that case, let's enjoy it together. I particularly like to watch the sunsets when I'm in Key West. They have a tradition there you know?" She looked into my eyes so intensely that I was having difficulty being the casual fellow I usually am, even with strangers.
 "Yes, I'd heard that. I just may drive down there for

Somewhere Along the Way

a few days while I'm here." We still hadn't introduced ourselves, so I held out my hand, "Derek Adams, and you are?"

"That's a very nice name. And you have strong hands, Derek. I'm pleased to make your acquaintance. My name is Constance Del Greco. Please call me Connie. All my friends do."

When a table became available, we moved to the patio where we could enjoy a slight breeze and be in a position to watch the fading sun sink slowly toward the horizon. I learned that Del Greco was her late husband's last name. He was her third husband, and she decided that he'd probably be the last. He died several years ago of a heart attack. Now she was enjoying a very active social life as a single person. She was frequently invited to parties. Having a proper escort had become a recent problem for her. I found that surprising, but didn't ask the obvious question. It would become answered in time, when she was ready.

"So, just what brings you to Miami, Derek?"

"I'm recently retired, recently divorced, and starting over. I started driving south and decided to browse around Miami for a few days just for the heck of it. And, I'm glad I did." I didn't feel like telling her the real reason I was in Miami, perhaps later. Trying to impress this woman would be futile. She'd heard it all. This lady walked to her own drumbeat and brought her own drums along.

"Well, I'm certainly glad, too. I think we should take a few days and visit Key West, so you won't think I was making that up, about the unusual sunsets there."

She quizzed me about my past, and I told her that I'd been in advertising for many years, working for several different ad agencies. There was a time when I thought I was creative, now I wasn't so sure. Finally I decided to start a second career, writing. I was working on my second novel, a murder mystery. While it took place in Detroit, the investigation expanded, allowing the detective to visit several other places to check on alibis. All this was true, and gave me a bonafide reason for making the trip to Miami. I could write off the expenses for the trip. I didn't bother to mention that my motel wasn't on the beach. Or the fact that my rental car was a budget model, mid-sized sedan.

"It sounds fascinating. Will you let me read the manuscript?"

"I have the first seven chapters finished. I'm re-editing several other chapters and may change some things around, depending on what I discover while I'm here." I was pleased that she seemed interested. Normally I don't discuss my writing activity until the manuscript is in finished form. Like many writers, I've always been sensitive to criticism.

"Does your detective have to stay in Miami? Or could he possibly be tempted to travel farther south, say to Key West?"

"Well, since I'm the creator of the story, I can allow my characters to travel just about anywhere that suits the circumstances. Key West might work out nicely. You'll see when you read the manuscript." I was thinking this could be a great way to meet again soon.

"Then it's settled. We're definitely going down to Key West to watch a few spectacular sunsets. Maybe it will provide some interesting background for your novel."

It had been a few years since I'd been back to The Keys and the idea appealed to me. I started thinking about the great shrimp I'd eaten there on my last trip. Also, the fantastic margaritas. Jimmy Buffett sure had the right idea on how to live. There was a man I truly admired. Maybe I'd become one of his Parrothead followers. It wouldn't take much convincing.

It was time to leave. The sun had done its thing, plopping down behind a row of commercial buildings and some palm trees. The crowd at the bar was beginning to get noisy and we could hardly talk. Connie appeared to have a little difficulty maneuvering around the table and took my arm for support. I began to worry about how drunk she might be. I was about to ask the old question, "your place, or mine" when she gave her ticket to the valet. He also seemed to know her.

"I think you'd better drive, if you don't mind." I'll bring you back tomorrow to get your car," she said. My question was answered before I ever asked.

Somewhere Along the Way

The valet arrived with her silver Jaguar convertible. The top was down, and we agreed to leave it that way and enjoy the sobering effects of the night's breeze.

"Where are you staying, Derek?" She asked. She was stroking my arm in a slow, but deliberate manner that I found pleasing. I'd give her a year to stop. If she could excite me that much just by stroking my arm, imagine what she might do to the rest of my aging body. It was a titillating thought. With some reluctance, I mentioned the name of the motel. We were not headed in that direction. I tried to remain within the speed limit, the last thing I needed was to be stopped right now. I didn't want any interruption that would spoil the sensuous moment.

The night air did indeed have a sobering effect. By the time we reached her place I was convinced I'd never find my way back to reality. The house was hidden from the road by a low brick wall and thick shrubbery. A button on the garage door opener, activated the wrought iron gates. Low lights illuminated the driveway to the house. It was a large two-story rambling house with a red tile roof. A covered carport sat back from the house, and when I pulled in I could see the pool beyond. It was a large estate, even though I couldn't see it all in the dark.

The grounds appeared to be well kept. We walked through another gate, and around the pool to a rear entrance. I waited while she deactivated the alarm system. When I turned to admire the pool, I noticed a sizeable yacht at the end of the dock beyond the pool. All I could think of was, why bother going to Key West? This was good enough for me, and any visiting dignitaries who might happen along.

"Mr. Del Greco left me a few bucks and this very nice house. I'll give you a tour in the morning. There are five guest rooms, so you can take your pick which one you prefer." Once again, it was that simple. No questions about my staying over, it had become a simple established fact, not a question to ponder. "You'll find everything you need in the bathroom, and in the closet. Just help yourself to whatever is there." She gave me the nickel tour of the first floor. "Care to take a dip in the pool before we hit the hay?" She was making herself another drink.

"I'm afraid I left my swimming trunks back at the motel."

"Oh pooh, you don't need any trunks. I skinny dip here all the time. But if you insist on modesty, you can find something in the cabana over there." She pointed beyond the pool. Once again my eyes riveted on the yacht. I couldn't determine its size in the dark, but it was big and beautiful.

"Is that yours, too?" I pointed at the yacht wondering just how rich this woman really was? And once again, why was she alone?

"Yes, but the young man who usually takes care of it quit recently, so I haven't taken it out for a while. Do you know anything about boats, Derek?"

"A little," I lied. I knew the front end was the bow, and the back end was the aft section. And I knew the big jobs like this had two engines, probably diesel, and could be difficult to start if you didn't know what you were doing. That was the total extent of my knowledge.

We pretended to swim, but mostly we just hugged and kissed in the water. She had a complete tan... all over. I on the other hand, had what is known as a golfer's tan and I was very conscious of how white I appeared next to her. Fortunately, she didn't seem to mind. Necking in the pool was exciting.

I managed to sleep until 8:30. I found a robe in the bathroom and all the shaving items in the cabinet. There was even a bottle of aspirin. When I finished my shower, a maid was making the bed. A large glass of fresh orange juice was on a tray on the dresser along with an envelope.

The note said she would meet me by the pool for lunch. Later, she would drive me back to get my car. Meanwhile, I was free to enjoy the pool and the house. The maid said that breakfast was ready downstairs. She was about 40, dark-skinned, spoke with an accent that might be Spanish, or Puerto Rican. She said her name was Lucy, and the cook's name was Emelda.

Somewhere Along the Way

After a fantastic breakfast, I read the paper with only passing interest. Then I wandered into the library and browsed an array of valuable first editions, many were signed copies. The house was a little too ornate for my taste. I couldn't determine if all the pictures were originals, or just good copies. Either way, the house gave the impression of old money.

The yacht turned out to be a 65- foot Viking. It had 2 staterooms. One had a king-size bed, the other was a queen-size. Each had their own bathroom complete with shower. The salon was equipped with an entertainment center that included a 56" color TV, stereo and a short wave radio station. All the wood was teak. I spent the better part of an hour admiring the yacht. Stereo speakers were everywhere. There were sleeping arrangements for a crew of three in a separate section behind the staterooms. Above, the galley had two refrigerators plus a separate freezer. Gourmet cookware was nicely stored in the cabinets. I had no idea what something like this would cost, but it had to be several million dollars at least. And here it was docked behind a mansion, hidden from the world. It was the kind of setting one might expect to see in a movie, not real life. And certainly not for just one person.

Connie had indicated earlier that she had never had any children. Her second husband, the one who had died from cancer, had two grown sons. Neither of them lived in Florida. So why did she need such a big estate? Maybe she threw some great parties? It was an interesting mystery I hoped to unravel before leaving.

"I see you discovered my late husband's favorite toy." She was seated by the pool as I returned from exploring the yacht. She looked beautiful, showing no signs of a hangover what so ever.

"It's absolutely beautiful... like everything else around here."

"Thank you. Yes, it is nice here. It gets a bit lonely at times, but never for very long." She smiled at me and motioned for me to sit beside her. "How about a Bloody Mary to get things started?"

I accepted. I also began to suspect that this woman drank a lot, more than I could ever hold. So I would be careful and pace my drinking. Over the years, I've known people who could drink all day and most of the night, and they seemed to hold it pretty well. I could never begin to do that, nor did I want to. In fact, there were many times when I preferred a soft drink rather than a beer when I was thirsty. My system would revolt if I thrust too many drinks in that direction.

"I'm glad you like it here. I have a suggestion to make. Why don't you bring your things from the motel and stay here? You can stay for as long as you plan to be in Miami. I enjoy your company. And, I was thinking of taking the boat down to Key West for a few days, rather than drive. Would you like that?"

Well who wouldn't like an offer like that? The decision was made before I even had a chance to say anything. My only worry was who would be driving that big yacht? Certainly not me! I told her that it was more boat than I felt comfortable handling.

"Don't worry. Ronaldo will be back. He will take us. If not, there are others who will be more than happy to go with us."

I thought back to that time when my teacher wanted each student to write about how they spent their summer. Who would ever believe how I was picked up? I no longer had the hard body of a 20-year old, my hair had turned gray and I was 60 years old. What would this glamorous woman see in somebody like me, when she could take her pick from hundreds of much better candidates? That was the question that was haunting me. Certainly she already had everything she could ever want. Maybe it was just some mature company, and intelligent conversation. That's just about all I had to offer. That, and my manuscript, if she remembered and was still interested in reading it.

After lunch by the pool, she gave me a tour of the estate, including the wine cellar that appeared to be well stocked. She knew much more about vintage wines than I did, so I kept quiet and just nodded occasionally. In the hallway, and in the living room there were quite a few photos of her when she was younger. She was equally beautiful then and had aged well.

"I used to be a model. That's how I met my first

husband. He owned a company that made ladies apparel that I modeled. I guess he liked what he saw."

"I thought all those companies were in New York, or Paris."

"Most of them are. We lived in New York for several years. He also had a place in Palm Springs. His mistress lives there now."

"What happened to him?" She hadn't mentioned him earlier, and I hadn't bothered to ask. This was a lady who decided when she would tell you something, and not a minute sooner. Rarely did she respond to a direct question.

"He disappeared. He was on a business trip in L.A. and never returned. The police never found him, dead, or alive. He simply vanished. You remind me of him in the way you smile and frown. You do that a lot, you know."

So that was it. I reminded her of her first husband who was probably killed by the mob, or something like that. Suddenly all this grandeur took on a different look. Each of her three husbands had been very rich, so she knew how to pick them.

"How long ago was it that he disappeared?" I wasn't sure I wanted too many details, and I doubted that she would provide much.

"We were married in New York in nineteen fifty-seven, and he disappeared sometime in April of fifty-nine. Almost two years after we were married. I hired a private investigator to look for him, but he never found anything, except my husband's mistress. I think he's living with her, or was, shortly after I fired him."

"You're the one who should be writing the murder mystery. You have all the ingredients for a good story."

"I suppose I have. I never thought about it that way. Why don't you use it for your next book?" She laughed when she saw that I was taking the idea quite seriously.

1959 was 45 years ago. If she was married in 1957, and assuming she was 20, or 21 then, that would make her at least 68 years old. She didn't look a day over 50. She must have found Gloria Swanson's secret for lasting beauty. Perhaps a plastic surgeon helped a little.

Richard Standring

She drove me back to Georgio's to get my rental car. I was surprised it was still there. She left for parts unknown while I returned to check out of my motel. We agreed to meet back at her place sometime later in the afternoon. That left me with some free time. The name on the yacht behind Connie's estate was *Wanderer*. I decided to check on its registration and ownership. The county court house would also have a recorded deed somewhere for the property. I could get the exact address from the Engineer's Dept. I also had the license plate number for her car. I was glad I had a few hours to play detective. I might use some of this in my book.

The yacht was registered to Halcyon Holdings, Ltd. I didn't have a clue who they were, but since her late husband had been a financial tycoon, I supposed it was one of his investments. More likely, a tax write off. The car was leased. And the property was deeded to Henderson Capital, a financial institution that listed its offices in The Cayman Islands. The mystery surrounding this woman seemed to intensify by the hour.

Nothing appeared to be in her name. For a second, I thought about the possibility that she was just a guest there. And once again, I began to feel apprehensive about staying there. Too much of a good thing never lasts, and the price is usually more than one expects. As an aging, retired, single man, I was scared. As a writer, looking for another story idea, I was intrigued. It was a bad combination, particularly when sex was a bonus, and I hadn't had much of that for a while.

"How was your afternoon?" she asked. I was sitting on the edge of the pool enjoying the breeze. This time, I had on swimming trunks.

"I did a little research for the book, then got lost trying to find my way back here," I said.

"Well, I'm glad you didn't get completely lost. I drove over to the marina, where Ronaldo hangs out, and left word that I needed him for a trip."

"Do you think he'll take us?" I half hoped he would turn her down, then we could drive. Or better yet, cancel the trip all together and stay here. There was nothing in Key West that would compare with this place. And, I secretly didn't give a shit about seeing another sunset while drinking a Margarita in some bar full of gays. Been there, done that and threw away the tee shirt. So why do it again? Probably because she wanted to, and she was the one establishing the agenda right now. I was just going along for the ride, Clyde.

"Oh yes, he knows better than to refuse me." She didn't elaborate, and I was afraid to inquire further what that meant. It did sound like a threat of sorts.

"So just what does this Ronaldo do? Is he a boat captain?"

"He does a lot of different things. He used to be my husband's bodyguard. He also acted as his chauffeur when it was necessary. And he handled taking care of the boat. He knows how to run it, and maintain it."

"Sounds like he has a lot of talent. Who does he work for now?"

"Do me a favor, Derek, don't ask too many questions about him. He is still under contract with my husband's firm. I use him whenever I need his services. He sometimes gets a little temperamental, particularly since my husband passed away. I told you that he quit, but that's not entirely true. We just had an argument over his using the boat. The only time I'll allow it to leave here, is when I'm on it. And I will be the one who determines where it will, or won't go. I guess he didn't like that, but he should have known better."

"Okay. I just like to know who is in charge of my life, and how good are they, while we're on the open water, far away from land, and all that good stuff." I tried to keep it on the light side, but I had some reservations about this individual, and I hadn't even met him yet. Being a bodyguard worried me.

"Don't be concerned. I only trust a few people. While Ronaldo and I may have a few differences, he respects who I am."

I wasn't sure what that meant, and I didn't need to know. "As long as you feel safe around this guy, I'm okay with him, too. I guess I'll have to be." I laughed to mask the serious aspect of what I'd just said.

We ate dinner on the yacht. Lucy brought everything out from the house. We dined on cold lobster salad, melon slices, black seedless grapes and key lime pie. We killed two bottles of white wine and watched an x-rated movie. I didn't need the movie to motivate my juices. We decided to spend the night on board so that I would get used to the boat and know where everything was kept. With the lights turned off, we were able to sit outside on the rear deck and watch all the stars.

In the distance, we could see a few of the houses on stilts in the bay area. Connie let it slip that Ronaldo lived in one of those houses. He had to use a speedboat to get to and from his house.

"They must cost a small fortune to own". I doubted that anyone who was a bodyguard and chauffeur could afford such a place. I hoped Ronaldo wasn't a member of some Columbian drug syndicate. I wanted no part of the drug trade, and that was running through my mind.

"I suppose so, I don't know what they cost. I guess I don't care," She curled close to me and fell asleep. I must have dozed off. When I woke, she was gone. I found her in the master stateroom sleeping. I wasn't ready for sleep, so I went back on deck and was surprised to see lights on in the house. It had been dark earlier. Perhaps the timers were messed up. I'd mention it to Connie in the morning so that she could reset them. Then, I distinctly heard a car drive down the driveway. With all I'd been told so far, I found it hard to go to sleep. Something strange was going on.

It was Friday, and I'd lost track of time. It was only 7:30 in the morning yet it seemed later than that. I'd forgotten that the sun seems to rise faster in the east when you're on the water. Connie was still sleeping when Lucy brought breakfast out to the boat. I could have made coffee, and for that matter, fixed breakfast from the galley, but she beat me to it. She also brought along the paper, keeping me occupied for the next hour.

"Is everything okay at the house?" I asked Lucy. The events of a few hours ago were still fresh in my mind.

"Yes, I think so. Is everything okay here?" she responded.

Somewhere Along the Way

"Couldn't be better. I thought I saw someone in the house last night. The lights came on very late, and I heard a car drive off later. That surprised me because I thought Connie, ah Mrs. Del Greco was the only one here."

"Sometimes the security people stop by to check on things. That's probably who it was." She didn't seem concerned, or upset. The explanation was logical enough, even though I still had doubts. Perhaps that's what happens when you start writing murder mysteries. You put yourself in the shoes of your main character, and start thinking like a detective. I had to admit the situation still scared me a little.

Just then Connie appeared, and Lucy hurried to pour her a glass of orange juice. She was wearing very revealing white silk pajamas. And even at 68, or however old she was, she filled them well. The woman knew how to walk, sit and even slouch gracefully.

"Lucy, tell Emelda to prepare something light for lunch. We'll be away for a few days. Just leave the answering machine on, and I'll check my messages, you don't have to bother with them."

As Lucy left, a striking young man in his late 20s was walking toward us. He wore a white golf shirt, khaki shorts and boat shoes. He was deeply tanned and the white shirt added to the contrast. He wore the widest smile I'd ever seen showing off a perfect set of teeth. This was obviously Ronaldo, and he could have had a job as a male model anywhere. He looked like a tennis pro and I instinctively sucked in my gut.

"See, you called, and I'm here. At your service as always." He bowed in an accented way that seemed a bit unnatural. When he turned to me and held out his hand, I saw the watch. It was an expensive Breitling Navigator, with 3 dials and several buttons. "I am Ronaldo, and you must be Connie's new guest." For some reason, he made it sound more like I was her latest one-night stand. Was he smiling, or grinning?

"Derek Adams. Pleased to meet you," was all I could manage. Ronaldo sized me up quickly.

"Well of course you are. Lucy informs me that the two of you spent the night out here. I trust you slept well?" Still grinning. He wasn't waiting for a reply, he moved forward to the console and started flipping switches. "We'll need to make a stop for some fuel." I didn't think he was talking to me since his back was to both of us.

"Let's plan on leaving in about an hour. I have a few things to get from the house before we leave, and I have a few calls to make." With that, Connie walked down the companionway in bare feet and pajamas looking very unconcerned.

"So what brings you to Miami, Derek?" Ronaldo was being very informal and certainly didn't act like hired help. He poured himself a cup of coffee and sat down in the lounge opposite me. The man exuded confidence.

"Just down for a few days. I'm working on a novel, and Connie suggested that Key West might provide some interesting background."

"Ever been to Key West before?"

"Yes, but it's been a few years. I understand there have been some changes and a lot of new construction."

"It's still a big tourist attraction. Connie loves to go there. I think it's because she gets so easily bored here. Difficult to imagine, isn't it? Having all this available, and still be bored." He shook his head in wonderment.

"I could probably get used to it," I said not wanting this conversation to go any further.

"So far, you've seen the pleasant side of Connie, because you're still here. I assure you, Derek, there's another side. She can be a real bitch when she wants to be. Take my advice, ignore her when she gets that way."

This had all the makings of a cruise to Hell. For an instant, I thought about just getting up and leaving. I had to go back to the house for my things anyway, I could just drive off and wave goodbye. Ronaldo was watching me carefully and I thought he must have read what I was thinking. He seemed to be nodding slightly, or was I imagining it? I left him sitting there using the phone and went to the house. I passed Lucy coming out of the kitchen with several baskets. No doubt lunch for an army.

When I returned to the boat, the engines were

idling. Ronaldo was in the cockpit at the controls, and there were two other Latin young men standing by ready to untie the ropes. A few minutes later, Connie appeared coming down the walkway. She was wearing white shorts, a green T-shirt and sandals. Her hair was pulled back and with the sunglasses, I would have thought it was a different, and much younger person. I helped her climb onboard, not that she needed any help. It was more a courteous gesture on my part. Ronaldo yelled something to the two young men and they untied the ropes, then jumped onboard. Apparently they were the crew. I hadn't thought about any others being with us.

Within a few minutes, we were in Biscayne Bay, traveling south. The shoreline remained in sight, and for some reason, that made me feel better.

For the next few hours, Ronaldo remained at the controls in the cockpit above, even though the boat was equipped with an autopilot. Connie was sun bathing on the forward deck in a next to nothing outfit in full view. She seemed totally unconcerned. I found a beer and relaxed in the lounge area and watched CNN on the large TV screen. Reception was better than I expected.

Late in the afternoon, we pulled into a marina at Marathon for fuel. Ronaldo said that we'd be here for an hour or so, and that one of his crew would remain onboard the ship at all times. I was free to walk around if I wanted. I waited around for Connie who was in the shower. She seemed to take a lot of time primping and applying make up. I suppose it's a woman thing. I offered to make her a martini, but she said she'd wait a bit. That too, surprised me.

While wandering around the marina, I heard some people complaining about how poor the fishing was. I hadn't even thought about fishing although Connie's boat was equipped with downriggers and a high watch tower, or whatever they called that crow's nest thing way up there along with all the antennas. Connie steered us to an outdoor bar that overlooked the marina where she ordered her first drink of the day. For once I was ahead of her.

"Are you enjoying the cruise?" she asked surveying the crowd as though she was looking for someone.

"Yes, it's quite pleasant. Ronaldo handles the boat well." I had the feeling he was quite competent at many skills.

"He's had a lot of experience. His father was a ship's captain for many years."

Taking her earlier advice, I didn't continue the conversation about Ronaldo. His crew of two managed to keep out of sight. They followed his commands, some of which were nothing more than hand signals, like soldiers. I was impressed, but didn't want to admit it.

"I was surprised to see land appear on our left, then I realized that we were traveling down the Intracoastal Waterway." I said this to get Connie's attention. We seemed to have run out of conversational subject matter. And I was afraid of becoming a boring guest.

"It is smoother and safer. Also a shorter distance this way. The ocean can become quite rough sometimes, even for a boat our size. Besides, I don't like being too far from shore should anything happen."

"I agree with you." And I did completely. So far, it really had been a comfortable and uncomplicated day. The weather was perfect. Visibility was good.

When we got back to the boat, there was a tray of freshly boiled shrimp on the table in the lounge. Connie and I snacked on the shrimp as Ronaldo pulled out into the waterway. We'd no doubt catch the sunset from the boat this evening, before arriving in Key West. An hour out from Marathon, Ronaldo appeared, handing the portable phone to Connie. She had a call. She took the phone and walked out to the rear deck without a word being said. I couldn't hear the conversation.

When she returned, she was wearing an angry expression. She ignored me, in fact walked past me, then down the steps to her stateroom. It's always an awkward moment when you're the guest. You see things and wonder, but you know not to ask any questions. I had the feeling that our pleasant day was about to have a different ending. I watched the spectacular sunset from the upper deck... alone. One of the crew was at the console. Ronaldo was somewhere below.

Once it became dark, everything appeared to be different. No horizon, a few lights from shore and thousands of stars overhead. The evening breeze was still warm, I didn't need my jacket. I wandered down below thinking I'd run into Ronaldo. As I came to the closed door outside Connie's forward stateroom, I heard what sounded like an argument.

"Don't think you can order me around," Connie yelled. Obviously she was having an argument with Ronaldo. I didn't want to be caught standing outside her door, so I entered the guest stateroom, where all my things had been deposited. I realized that we had not bothered with dinner. The shrimp had been sufficient for me, but I was never the less surprised that it hadn't been mentioned. We hadn't spoken much since we left South Miami. And, she hadn't bothered to ask about the manuscript, even though I had it with me. Accepting her invitation had been a mistake. Now, perhaps the best thing to do would be to leave at the earliest convenient time. It wouldn't upset Ronaldo.

I heard a door close and footsteps in the hallway. I waited a few minutes, then went out into the empty hallway and knocked softly on Connie's door.

"Leave me alone!" was her response through the closed door.

"Connie it's Derek. Are you alright?"

"I said, leave me alone. I'll talk with you in the morning." I didn't like the thought of sharing the evening with Ronaldo, but had no choice.

Being left to my own devices, I went into the galley and searched for something to eat. I found a box of cold baked chicken legs. I put several into a plastic bag and popped them into the microwave. A few minutes later I was satisfied. Ronaldo appeared while I was still sitting at the dinette. He had a drink in his hand.

"I see you managed to find something to eat." He wasn't being overly cordial, nor was he smiling. He moved into the booth and sat down facing me.

"Is Connie okay?" I asked.

"She's not feeling well. Too much sun I think. She spends a lot of time in the sun, and she drinks too much. A bad combination for a woman her age."

"I think she looks pretty good, all things considered."

"Well yes, I suppose you would say that. You're just a little younger than she is. I must tell you, she usually picks up younger men than you." It was a stinging put down. I let it slide, Clyde.

"You mean, men more your age?"

"Exactly. She loves to be escorted by handsome young men. She's a little vain about appearances."

"And were you ever one of those escorts?" I knew I shouldn't have asked, but it just slipped out because I was angry. And because I was just another temporary guest invited along for her pleasure. I wasn't comfortable in the role of gigolo, yet that's what it must have appeared to be.

"Don't concern yourself, Derek, with who I am, or what I am. It's none of your business. And, I'm afraid I have some bad news for you. We won't be going to Key West after all. We are stopping at another key for a few days, to make some needed repairs. I'm sure you'll be able to get a ride back to Miami from there."

"I see. How soon 'till we reach our new destination?" I wasn't overly upset with the news, but I tried to look disappointed. Something was wrong, and it wasn't with the boat. That was just a convenient excuse to put me ashore, which was fine with me. I had contemplated that once we reached Key West, things might change. I knew I could catch a commuter flight from either Key West, or Marathon, back to Miami easy enough.

"We'll be there within the hour. I suggest you get your things ready. And please don't disturb Mrs. Del Greco. She's sleeping." It was the first time he had referred to her formally. I was being officially dismissed.

We pulled into the harbor area of Big Pine Key. The rubber motor launch that was secured to the top deck was now in the water waiting for me. Both of Ronaldo's crew were there, one in the boat, the other holding a line. Ronaldo called to me from the top deck looking down.

"Have a safe trip back, Derek. There is a ride waiting on shore for you. He will drive you back to Marathon." With that the outboard motor went into high revolutions and we danced across the bay to the pier. It was a short ride and I wondered why Ronaldo elected to remain anchored in the bay, if indeed he was there for repairs? Why not pull directly into the dock?

I asked the driver to wait around a few minutes. I told him that I wanted to be sure the launch returned safely before we departed. Actually I just wanted to see if the yacht would remain there, or leave. It left as I suspected it would.

"So what are your instructions?" I asked the driver. We were riding in an older model pickup truck.

"I'll be dropping you off at the Howard Johnson motel. They have a room waiting for you. You're lucky, because they are always full this time of year."

"Who made the reservations? You?"

"I don't know who made them. Don't ask me any questions. I don't know anything. I just do what I'm told. They told me to pick you up and take you to the motel, and that's what I'm doing."

"So who do you work for?" He never answered my question, just shook his head.

The motel room was reserved in my name and already paid for. The desk clerk handed me an envelope with my name on it, along with the room key.

The driver was right, the motel was full. When I opened the envelope, there was a note from Connie along with $500.

> *Derek,*
> *Please don't be angry with me. I'm sorry things didn't work out as planned. I trust this will cover any unexpected expenses.*
> *C D G*

All these arrangements must have been made while we stopped for fuel. I had no way of knowing if the note was actually from Connie, or written by someone else. I had already been warned not to ask too many questions, and this was just one more of a long list I had. Right now, this aging, poorly- equipped gigolo was happy to still be in one piece, dry, and able to write about the strange events that took place while visiting South Miami.

Maybe it would be a sequel to my murder mystery. It was time for me to check on those alibis of my suspects

Richard Standring

in the story, that somehow became almost forgotten. Were the events of the last two days stranger than fiction? You bet they were.

I'd have to tell my friend, the one who recommended Georgio's, that it was a most unusual place. As a result, I'd met several unforgettable people. I'll probably include a few in my novel; the one Connie never bothered to read.

For the next few days, I kept thinking about famous writers like Truman Capote and Ernest "Papa" Hemingway. Both had lived in Key West and hung out in the bars, meeting all sorts of interesting, colorful characters. At least we had that in common.

End

Somewhere Along the Way

Richard Standring

Crackistan

He told me, he was the Prime Minister,
From the Altered States of Crackistan.
All his followers worshipped his cause.
For them, he was *The Man*.

Crackistanies have this weird belief,
That life can be great... for a little while.
If you buy into that story,
You'll make the Prime Minister smile.

The price for a trip to his promised land,
Is more than anyone should pay.
When I said I wasn't interested,
He laughed, "Perhaps another day".

Crackistan is a mythical place,
Not somewhere one needs to go.
Too many have gone there already,
As the Prime Minister's records show.

The Altered States of Crackistan,
Awaits the young, weak and unwary.
Just let the temptation pass you by,
A trap, and a trip, that's unnecessary.

        RAS

Somewhere Along the Way

Richard Standring

THE PITCHMAN'S DANCE

"Good morning ladies and gentlemen. My name is Jerry, and for the next ninety minutes, I'm going to reveal to you some facts that might just change the way you currently think and feel about computers." The speaker stood in front of a group of approximately two hundred people of various ages. They had just finished a free continental breakfast and were now obligated to listen and watch a brief, ninety-minute presentation.

I kept thinking, if it sounds too good to be true, then it's either a scam, or they're selling something really expensive. Over the years, I'd heard and seen my fair share of presentations. Usually the presenter was a trained professional who knew how to work the audience. They could walk the walk and talk the talk. This fellow fit the profile. He was good looking, in his early to mid-30s, took off his suit jacket soon after being introduced. He had a clip-on mini mike that left both hands free for frequent gestures, not unlike a preacher delivering a sermon. I knew Jerry planned to take off his jacket because his nametag, with large bold block letters, was affixed to his shirt, just above the pocket. I wondered if anyone else had picked up on this subtle trick. Everyone in the room wore a similar nametag with just a first name, large enough for Jerry to read from a distance as he moved around the room.

"How is everyone this morning?" he asked. The response was weak.

"Hey, in a few minutes, when I ask you that question again, I'll bet I hear some yelling and cheering. If you asked me that question, I'd yell GREAT!" He almost shouted. "Okay, let's get started here. How many of you consider yourselves to be computer literate? Raise your hands." A few hands went up.

"And how many of you would like to be computer literate? Raise your hands." Quite a few hands went up

Somewhere Along the Way

this time.

"Now, how many of you currently own a computer in your home?" A few hands went up. I noticed he was doing a quick count and made a slight nod to someone in the rear of the room.

"And finally, how many of you never like to raise your hand? Raise your hand." That got a few laughs and a few raised hands. He was getting everyone loosened up. "I'm here to tell you that if you want to be successful in the new millennium, you'll have to be computer literate and computer active. Anyone here want to dispute that fact?" No hands, no one spoke. He let that sink in while he slowly surveyed the crowd. Then he picked out a woman in the second row. "Alicia, I noticed that you don't have a computer. I'll bet you'd like to have one and be able to use it every day, wouldn't you?" She nodded yes.

"And you, Robert, I'll bet that even though you already have a computer, you'd like to be able to use it to full advantage, isn't that right?" Another nod.

"Okay, now all of you who currently own a computer, how many of you use the Internet for shopping and getting useful information?" A few hands shot up.

"Good. You've got a head start on the rest of the folks here, but listen up because even you will benefit from what I'm going to say."

I had a feeling the pitch was about to begin. This man with the well-modulated voice was sweeping the room left to right, then right to left again. His eyes were gathering information while his arms were open wide and he was smiling. He had perfect teeth. He'd done this routine so often that his body was a robot. The words were preprogrammed, leaving his brain to calculate how many in the audience would be responsive to his later proposal. For the pitch to be truly effective, he had to work up to the precise moment, making them want it, whatever that was. It was almost like teasing a child, holding a piece of candy just out of reach.

A four-color slide was projected onto a screen behind him with his name and the company name, Universal Learning Systems, LLC. An email address was below the logo. As Jerry spoke, he clicked a small remote, changing the slides as he showed a series of people and quotes, all praising the benefits they'd received from Universal. After six examples, Jerry shifted to the next phase. These were typical screens of various Internet providers followed by a series of web sites. "This probably looks confusing to you right now, but I assure you that it won't be long before they will be familiar to you. You'll be searching for job opportuneities, reading your horoscopes, maybe finding a new love interest, chatting with others who share the same hobbies as you, or just learning some additional facts. Let me give you an example. You will have an encyclopedia of data available to you... twenty-four hours a day. How many of you have a current set of encyclopedias at home right now? Raise your hand." No hands were raised.

"Marge, what do you think a good set of encyclopedias go for today?" She didn't seem to have any idea. "Would you think about fifteen hundred dollars?" She nodded agreement. "Folks that's just one of thousands of benefits you get from having a computer in your home, available to you any time you want to use it. Have a medical question? You can get answers fast with your computer. Suppose you are looking for a new home. You can browse what's available without ever leaving home, or getting dressed. Saves a lot of time, and you don't have to listen to a salesperson yapping at you every minute. Those are just some of the benefits. There are a lot more. You can save on postage and reduce your long distance phone bills to nothing. How many of you would like to do that? Raise your hand." Quite a few hands flew up.

"Now write this down on the pad in front of you. Starting today, the way I live is about to change for the better." Everyone was writing as instructed. I recognized the technique of getting audience participation.

"In a minute, my lovely assistant back there is going to pass out an information sheet. Be sure to fill out the top part, so we'll know more about you. From time to time, we make special offers to those who attend our seminars, saving you some serious money. That's why we want you to have that same opportunity. We don't sell your name to any other company, I promise you that, so there's no need to worry." When a salesman tells me that, it's usually a signal to start worrying.

I was already on alert and ready for the next step toward the close. I looked at my watch. We'd been captivated by Jerry for a total of eighty-five minutes. He'd promised ninety, so we were getting pretty close to the end. This was a man who kept to a timed schedule, so I doubted that we would go past the allotted time, unless there were questions.

"Now, on the reverse side, you'll see that we've listed the price for our primary computer course. Don't let that seven hundred and fifty dollars scare you. While it's worth every penny, because you are here today, we're making you a special offer. We are practically giving the course away at the ridiculous price of only ninety-nine fifty. That's a six hundred and fifty dollar savings, folks.

"Look down the page and you'll see that we're also offering you a complete computer package with all the software installed, ready for you to start practicing and surfing the Internet. You can't buy a system like this in any store for less than three thousand dollars. So, cross out that three thousand dollar amount and write special one-time offer.

"Now are you ready of this?" He waited, watching how everyone was poised, anticipating the new low price. "Put down... fourteen hundred and thirty dollars. That's right. Some of you look surprised, and you should be. For a total of fifteen hundred twenty-nine dollars and fifty cents, you'll receive the complete course, the computer system and software delivered to you. You won't even have to pay the freight. There is one catch. You knew there was a catch, didn't you?" Heads nodded.

"We can't offer you this special computer with all the extra features unless you also agree to the course. The two items are designed to go together."

"Can we buy just the course?" someone in the group asked.

"Ordinarily no. But I feel certain that you'll be so pleased with the course that you'll tell all your friends about it, and we'll sell it to them for seven hundred. Hah ha," he laughed at this and winked. "Sure, I'll sell you the course. I'm here today to help you, not to give anyone a hard time. And to make it easy for you, just jot down at the bottom of the page the best payment method you prefer to use. You can charge this to your credit card, or write a check, whatever you decide is okay with me.

"Now, for the first dozen of you that order today, we'll give you the course to take home with you. We'll ship your system to you within the week. That's it for me, unless you have questions." He looked at his watch and I looked at mine. Ninety minutes on the button. He'd allowed time for that one question.

"Just give your order sheets to Debby in the back of the room before you leave." Jerry started to unhook his mini mike and turn off the projector. At least half the room was cuing up in a line for the table in the rear of the room. As I approached the exit, I looked at the table and counted what appeared to be at least four dozen shrink-wrapped boxes. Everyone signing up would be going home with a course, not just the first dozen.

This was an impulse pitch. Well planned and orchestrated to create desire, appealing to those who thought they were saving a great deal of money. As I left the Holiday Inn, I drove past Radio Shack and decided to do some comparison shopping. I found a similar system for eleven hundred dollars. A few days later, a computer catalog arrived in the mail. I found another similar system listed for nine hundred dollars. The pitchman's dance had lasted ninety minutes. Even if I didn't buy his act, at least it was entertaining. The coffee and rolls were free... just like the advice I remembered hearing, "If it sounds too good to be true...."

A week later, I was shopping in a large supermarket and heard an announcement over the public address system. "Attention shoppers, there will be a free demonstration in aisle five. For all those interested, they will be giving away a free gift, just for watching a brief demonstration."

Once again, I was intrigued enough to wander over

Somewhere Along the Way

to the designated area where there were a few dozen people with shopping carts assembled around a raised area. This time the pitch was for a vegetable chopper and instant salad maker. The clip-on mike helped free up the man's busy hands. He watched the audience while he spoke in a well-rehearsed monologue. The only time he asked the crowd to raise their hand, was at the end, when he made the offer. It was a quick five-minute show, after which they passed out small paring knives.

I thought back to an earlier time when medicine men roamed the countryside peddling concoctions guaranteed to eliminate dozens of health related problems, grow hair, remove warts and allow you to have a peaceful night's sleep.

Later, I watched a TV commercial for something guaranteed to eliminate acid indigestion. In fine print there was a message indicating that the person in the demonstration wasn't a real doctor, and that some side-affects could occur under a variety of conditions. This time, nobody asked me to raise my hand.

End

Richard Standring

LEGENDS, MYTHS, FOLKTALES & SPOOKY STUFF

"Once upon a time, a long time ago..." the old man starts telling a story, staring into the flickering fire. His mind is going back to another time and place. He is about to relate a tale that was told to him, many years hence. And now, it is time for him to pass on the story to those gathered around him. His words come out slowly and softly.

Young and old sit quietly, huddled close together, listening with sharply tuned ears. They don't want to miss a word. Darkness provides a contrasting backdrop of apprehension and mystery for the scary story they are about to hear. Fear of the unknown makes them a captive audience, as they become mesmerized by the unfolding tale. In this atmosphere, the unbelievable suddenly becomes believable.

This setting could be a band of gypsies sitting around a campfire, somewhere in Medieval Europe. It could be a tribe of Indians listening to legends about their ancestors. Or, in modern times, it could be a group of Boy Scouts listening to a ghost story. It could even be a few cowhands out on the range, listening to the old-timer tell about a lost gold mine in the faraway hills. For centuries, stories (myths, legends and folktales) have been retold around similar campfires.

Because we are better educated today, and have the benefit of modern science, most of these stories serve as entertainment. Yet there are still some phenomena, like: UFOs, The Bermuda Triangle, The Loch Ness Monster and The Abominable Snowman, to name a few, that continue to mystify us. The search for the lost continent of Atlantis is ongoing. Someday, we may know the answers that have so far eluded scientific inquiry.

Somewhere Along the Way

Meanwhile, they are the source for many good tales. Who can say if they exist? That point alone makes them all the more interesting. Is Big Foot real, or imagined? And, did the Druids actually lift and carry all those huge, heavy stones to create Stonehenge? They must have taken a few lessons from the Egyptians, who mastered the art of stone construction without using heavy equipment.

Whenever a situation occurs that can't be adequately explained, a myth will eventually develop. Someone is expected to know the answer. In ancient times, the response was a sacrifice to the gods. Earthquakes, volcanic eruptions, tidal waves and terrible storms occurred then, as they do now. Today, we know that an eclipse of the moon is not an uncommon event to be feared. 3,000 years ago, people were no doubt horrified. Greek and Roman mythology set the stage for establishing answers for unusual situations. Gods like Zeus, Apollo, Hercules, Poseidon and Venus had to be appeased. Those in higher authority used mythology as a means for control, providing convenient answers. Who would dare challenge the wishes of the gods?

For centuries, legends and myths were told by passing minstrels, balladeers, troubadours, court jesters, gypsies, shaman, witch doctors and even medicine men. No doubt the stories became exaggerated over time, as they were passed on. They were all created to serve a purpose: To scare, entertain, create an illusion, or establish a desired conclusion. While the Hunchback of Notre Dame never really existed, many believe the story to be true. It was a time when the Catholic Church wanted to re-establish a dwindling attendance. Camelot, Merlin and good old Robin Hood materialized as other legends.

The twentieth century has embraced some interesting stories like: The Legend of Sleepy Hollow (and the headless horseman), legends of lost gold mines, ghost ships, pirates and haunted houses. And, a few monsters were created along the way. We've been scared by Frankenstein, The Wolf Man, Dracula, King Kong and more recently by Stephen King. Television has added some newer versions. The old Boogie Man has taken on

Richard Standring

a few new appearances, wearing a hockey mask, a Darth Vader helmet, or a gruesome monster with horns.

The enchanted world of make believe has entertained, (not scared), children with delightful creations from Sesame Street and Walt Disney. Howdy Doody, Lamb Chop, Barney and Pooh Bear became bedtime companions. Children of all ages have been able to enjoy the recreations of stories like: Alice in Wonderland, Beauty and the Beast, Little Red Riding Hood, Jack and the Bean Stalk, Peter Pan, Snow White and the Seven Dwarfs, and Pinocchio. Prior to the advent of television, fairy tales were usually read as bedtime stories ending with, "...*And they all lived happily ever after*".

Back to the spooky stuff -- Prior to television, radio provided a good medium for scary episodes from programs like: The Inner Sanctum, The Shadow, The Mysterious Traveler and Lights Out. Campfire stories and folktales will never be replaced by television. Our imagination needs a different atmosphere to take us to that other place... beyond the sparks of the dying embers. To shiver when a lone wolf howls in the darkness and an owl responds, as clouds drift across a full moon. We're startled when we hear the snap of a broken branch, as we try to fall asleep with all those scary images. We remember them vividly, so they can be retold at another time.

The art of story telling will live on, even as technology changes. New monsters will be created. New mysteries will materialize. Hopefully, with the help of storytellers, the old ones will never be forgotten.

End

Somewhere Along the Way

Richard Standring

What Tomorrow Brings

"Be careful tomorrow," the fortune teller advised in a low, soft voice. Irmadene Caldwell had an entire lexicon of generic phrases she used that could apply to almost anyone, or any situation. She always ended a *session* with one of these ambiguous generalizations.

Most of Irmadene's clients were older women, and most were worrying about the same things: Their health, their grandchildren and the future in general. Most were widows living on the limited income Social Security provided. Therefore Irmadene had to keep her price at ten dollars per session. Each session was never lasted more than twenty minutes.

Once in a while a stranger would venture into her home. This always caused her a bit of apprehension because the Better Business Bureau had recently issued an advisory against her establishment, indicating she was a fraud, offering nothing more than a few minutes of sympathetic conversation. The last part was true.

What the Better Business Bureau didn't know was that Irmadene, a.k.a. Jasmine before moving to Cedar Bluff ten years earlier, was a keen observer, thus she was able to pinpoint a client's concern and ask appropriate questions. The answers provided the roadmap to where the session would eventually end.

"I see you're having trouble sleeping," she told one customer with dark circles under her eyes. It was obvious enough, even in the dimly lit room.

"Yes I am," the older lady replied. "I wake up worrying about my grandson."

"He's been a concern to you for some time."

"Yes! How did you know that?"

"I see many things when we're together like this. Tell me, how old is your grandson?"

"He's eight. He'll be nine next month. His step-father promised to bring him for a week-end stay, but he

97

keeps delaying. It's a different excuse each week."

"And you're not sure how sincere he is. You're wondering why he's keeping your grandson from seeing you."

"Yes! That's what's troubling me. Finally someone understands my problem."

"And how is your daughter?" Irmadene kept file cards on each of her regular clients with detailed information. She always reviewed a file card just prior to a session, so she could appear interested and knowledgeable about that person's situation. Irmadene learned this trick when she was still a hairdresser.

Twenty years and a hundred and fifty pounds later, Irmadene had trouble standing on her feet too long. She wore house slippers and a loose-fitting sleeveless sundress. Her one item of ornamentation was a fake gold chain with a large cut glass pendant the size of a silver dollar. Each facet of the pendant would reflect flickers of light from burning scented candles. The pendant was her subtle replacement for a crystal ball, so she always wore it when she was giving a session.

Customers frequently seemed mesmerized by the pendant against a backdrop of her 44D bosom. The women focused on the pendant, while the men looked slightly beyond. Nobody seemed to notice the house slippers or her swollen ankles. They remained below the table, therefore she never considered them to be anyone's concern. Occasionally she had to use her cane to walk.

The trick was to be a good listener and interject key questions at the proper time, always expressing an interest. There were times when she had to be careful not to stifle a yawn. A wall clock in the kitchen was visible through a partially open door. From her side of the small round table in the dining room, she could look directly at a customer and glance beyond to see how much time was left without displaying any impatience.

Irmadene once read that all the great magicians agreed, *it was just show business.* She applied that theory to her present activities and for the most part, she had a cadre of satisfied clients who came to her on a regularly scheduled basis, just as they would if they were getting their hair done.

Another trick Irmadene regularly used was reading the daily horoscopes of those she planned to see. It paid to be in sync with the stars. She didn't read palms, cards or tea leaves. She just sat across the table, sometimes holding outstretched hands of her client. All the while, listening and watching for a cue to ask a question or make a generic statement that couldn't be challenged.

After all, everyone had to be careful tomorrow. No one really knew what tomorrow might bring. She just made hints and allowed her clients to make their own interpretation.

Martha Cooper Alderdice scheduled her weekly visit to Irmadene's on Fridays, just before going grocery shopping. Then while shopping, she'd ponder what she learned from *her spiritual counselor*. Irmadene never actually called herself by that title, it was just something Martha used as a way of categorizing Irmadene from her other acquaintances. She stopped discussing her visits with her bridge friends because of their snickering.

A widow for seven years, Martha wondered if she'd ever find someone else to spend the rest of her days with? She was sixty-six, lived alone in a big house on Maple Street in a nice neighborhood. She knew the prospects of finding an eligible, healthy, single gentleman in Cedar Bluff were pretty slim. There were many more single women than men in her age group and national statistics confirmed that. However, Irmadene had hinted, "There is someone interested in you".

The next few days, following that visit to Irmadene's, Martha took particular notice of every male that smiled, or spoke, to her. The mailman always smiled, but he was considerably younger and married, that ruled him out as a candidate.

Sam, the butcher at the supermarket, always smiled, but then he smiled at everyone. That week, Martha returned more smiles than she could ever remember. Consequently, it was a pleasant week, seeing everyday acquaintances and neighbors, but the one

Somewhere Along the Way

person she was seeking never materialized.

"You need to be patient in your searching," Irmadene advised at their next session. Martha reminded her she was getting old fast, and time was running out. If she was to find that special someone, it had to be soon. As she said that, Irmadene turned slightly and there was a flash of light reflected in the jeweled pendant hanging around Irmadene's neck. Martha knew it was a sign that something exciting was about to happen. Irmadene ended the session with, "Tomorrow will be full of surprises."

Later that afternoon, Martha's water heater quit working. She called several plumbers before finding someone who could replace it on Saturday. The listing in the newspaper said he did home maintenance repairs.

When *The House Doctor* arrived, Martha had momentarily forgotten about her search. She was more concerned about having hot water again. Standing on the front porch was a handsome older man with white hair and a big smile on his leathered, clean-shaven face. He looked to be at least six feet tall and near her age.

"I'm here to fix your problem," he said, "and any other items that need attention."

Why Martha had baked an apple pie earlier, was something she couldn't explain. She was just taking it out of the oven when the handyman arrived.

"Can I interest you in a cup of coffee and a warm piece of apple pie?"

"You sure can," he replied stepping inside the big old house.

That was the day Martha Cooper Alderdice met her older Prince Charming. He'd arrived at a time when she wasn't actually searching.

The moment the handiman stepped inside her house, Martha felt tingles all over and instantly knew her new sole mate, the one she hoped to find, had arrived.

She credited Irmadene for knowing what her future would be. No one would ever convince Martha otherwise.

End

Richard Standring

A Distant Drum

At a recent dinner party, the conversation turned to past events and experiences. Our host asked, had any of us ever saved someone's life?

Bryan Hartford immediately emerged from a distant and suppressed memory. I hadn't thought about him in years. Now suddenly he was back, occupying my thoughts. When I first met Bryan, he was the marketing manager for Hamilton Security Systems. I was the advertising account person who helped win Hamilton's business with a presentation that fortunately appealed to Bryan and his boss, Lee Hamilton, founder and CEO of the company. That's how we met.

It wasn't long into our new relationship when I learned that Bryan was an accomplished drummer. He and two friends played a regular gig every weekend in Shadyside at an upscale lounge coincidently called *The Shady Side*. In those days, Shadyside was to Pittsburgh, what Greenwich Village is to New York City. It was the in place to hang out in the '60s. Bryan's trio drew a regular crowd every Friday and Saturday evening and I soon became another of Bryan's fans.

It didn't take long before I noticed that Bryan always had several attractive females keeping him company during his frequent breaks. He appeared to be a real lady's man. The broad smile on his face as he shared a cigarette with one of the ladies said it all.

Because Hamilton was a small company, Bryan's primary responsibilities involved dealer sales. Marketing was more of a title than an activity and I began spending more time with Lee Hamilton. Bryan didn't seem to mind. Lee's lifelong best friend, Walt Powell, was vice president of sales. Like Bryan, Walt was always busy negotiating for a big industrial contract somewhere and didn't appear to have much interest in the advertising. That surprised me since Walt was Bryan's immediate supervisor, yet neither of them

Somewhere Along the Way

attempted to get involved. It actually made my job a lot simpler having just one person approve the ideas rather than a committee, which too often delays the process.

Lee Hamilton was one of the most charismatic people I'd ever met. I learned that during WWII, he was a highly decorated fighter pilot and an Ace in the European theatre. One wall in his office displayed his numerous medals, along with photos of him with famous movie stars and celebrities. He was married to Marsha Bromfield, the daughter of steel magnate, Cyrus Bromfield. Over time, I learned that it was Cyrus who loaned Lee the money to start the company, which became an overnight success once the Bromfield connection was made.

Marsha's photo was prominently displayed on the console behind Lee's Brazilian walnut desk. She was as beautiful as any of the female movie stars on the wall. It occurred to me that Lee was indeed fortunate to be married to a rich and beautiful woman and having a powerful father-in-law in his corner. What more could any successful businessman ever want? Lee seemed to have it all and to have done it all. I admired him.

Since most of our meetings were conducted over lunch, at the nearby country club, I always heard a few chapters about Lee's many war adventures. He'd had a fascinating flying career and had been shot down six times, but never captured. Walt and Bryan would join us for lunch then excuse themselves early, having heard these stories before.

Lee reminded me a lot of the older movie star Errol Flynn. Like most adventurers who'd done it all, he was also an accomplished drinker. He could handle a three Martini lunch while I stayed with just one. It was during one of those long lunches that Lee invited me to go with him to New York City to attend a security equipment trade show. Then he dropped the bomb. The decision to attend the show was a last-minute idea, and now he needed to decorate a booth displaying the company's product line. It had to be tasteful and project the proper image. And, it had to be completed and in New York in three weeks!

It was an impossible request, yet I managed to pull

it off somehow, winning Lee's admiration along the way. Whenever I had Lee's approval on something, I noticed that Walt would manage to make a negative comment later. I mentioned this observation to Bryan on a Saturday night during one of his breaks.

"Walt doesn't like anyone to get too close to Lee. The fact that Lee likes you, is reason enough for him to take a negative position. That's just the way he is," Bryan explained. With that he finished off his drink, stubbed out his cigarette and returned to his drums, blending in with the piano and bass without missing a beat. The man didn't have to sell security systems, he could make a living with his music.

My reward for meeting Lee's deadline was three long, work-filled days in New York. Bryan and I shared a room at The Plaza. Lee and Walt shared a suite on a different floor. The first night we hit a half dozen well-known night spots. On two occasions Bryan was recognized and asked to sit in on one of the sets. Following each of his brief performances, he was rewarded with female companions. They seemed to materialize from the crowd. Bryan was that kind of magnet and we briefly basked in his celebrity. Even Walt seemed impressed.

"Hang around Bryan long enough and you're sure to get lucky," Lee advised. I wondered if that charm was one of his hidden assets in the company.

The second night, Bryan said he had a date, leaving Lee, Walt and me to dine and drink alone. Walt soon followed, leaving me to keep Lee company and make sure he got back to the hotel safely. I knew I had to be the one to remain reasonably sober.

"I need a special favor," Lee asked while on his sixth or seventh drink, I wasn't counting. We'd just finished a superb meal, but I wasn't used to eating so late.

"Sure. Just ask, and I'll do whatever you want," I said, wondering just what he could possibly need from me. So far I was batting a thousand with the booth being a big hit. I wasn't expecting another surprise.

"Listen carefully. I'm not as drunk as you might think I am, and this is very important. I need you to leave your hotel room door unlocked tonight."

"You want me to do what?" I was instantly apprehensive.

"I'm going to swear you to secrecy on this." When I nodded, he continued. "Bryan is about to make a six-story fall out the window."

"That doesn't make any sense to me at all. He's not the type to commit suicide."

"You're right, he's not, but I'm going to change that. I'm going to help Bryan go out the window. And it will look like a suicide."

"Whatever for?" I couldn't believe what I was hearing. I became instantly sober.

"Bryan is having an affair with my wife. I found out three weeks ago." It suddenly occurred to me that was about the time the decision was made to attend this trade show.

"Have you confronted him about this?" I asked.

"No, he doesn't know that I know, but he is worried that I might suspect something. He didn't want to come on this trip. He tried to beg off with several different excuses."

Lee proceeded to explain how it happened. It was a Friday, and usually the three of them, Lee, Walt and Bryan had lunch together and discussed a variety of things going on at the plant, as well as their respective schedules for the next week. Only this Friday, Bryan left soon after eating. He explained he was meeting someone. Two hours later, back at the office, Bryan was still gone and Lee wanted to discuss a few things with him. He suspected Bryan might be shacked up with somebody, so Lee drove past several nearby motels looking for Bryan's company car; a Pontiac station wagon, so he could haul his drums around.

It didn't take long before Lee spotted Bryan's station wagon hidden behind a motel where it couldn't be seen from the highway. Lee pulled in and parked beside the station wagon and knocked on the motel room door. Bryan opened the door a few inches. He was wearing just his boxer shorts. Bryan muttered something to the effect that he'd be back in the office in about an hour. Before closing the door, Lee noticed his wife's Russian Sable coat draped over a chair. The fur coat had an unusual red silk lining. As Bryan closed the door, Lee felt his life evaporating and wondered how such a good friend could do this to him. Lee returned to the office and waited for Bryan who never made it back.

To eliminate any doubt, Lee called his house and spoke to the housekeeper who confirmed that Mrs. Hamilton was out for the afternoon, presumably playing bridge at the country club. Just to cover all bases, Lee drove back to the country club and found his wife's car, but she was nowhere to be found. The man who had it all, who had faced death during the war, was now confronted with a crisis. A divorce would be costly. He could lose control of the company. Lee was devastated, yet he couldn't bring himself to confront either Bryan or his wife. He had to find a quick solution to eliminate the problem.

Lee and Bryan had been friends for 20 years. Lee knew that Bryan had his choice of women. And he was married to a delightful lady and they had two young children. Lee knew that Bryan fooled around and joked that it was be a musician's perk. I had to agree with that assessment, having seen Bryan in action at *The Shady Side*.

Lee's plan was to kill Bryan while in New York. Walt would be Lee's alibi that he was in their suite when the incident happened. All I had to do was report discovering the window open when I returned to our room.

Eventually it hit me that I would be an accomplice to murder regardless, and I didn't want any of this to happen. I tried to talk Lee into confronting Bryan and maybe working something out. In my opinion, murder wasn't the solution to the problem. If Bryan was a Casanova, then he obviously wasn't in love with any of the women he was fooling around with... including Marsha Bromfield Hamilton. It was just a momentary fling at best. Lee didn't see it that way.

It was 2:30 A.M. when we arrived back at The Plaza through a kitchen entrance, so the doorman wouldn't see us arrive. I took the elevator up to the sixth floor, fumbled with my key and rushed into the room making as much noise as I could. Bryan remained asleep snoring loudly. I shook him awake telling him he had to get up, get dressed and get out... immediately! He didn't seem to understand what I was saying. I slowed down and repeated the message.

"Lee knows about you and Marsha! He's planning to kill you, Bryan. You have to get out of here right now, before Lee shows up, or you're a dead man!"

"What? Oh my God, he knows? That explains why he was acting a little strange tonight. I guess I really screwed up this time. I've got to alert Marsha right away. I don't know what she'll want to do. If he wants to kill me, he might want to harm her as well. There's a dangerous side to Lee that you don't know anything about," he said.

"And I don't want to know, either," I replied.

By 3:00 A.M. Bryan was gone. He caught an early flight back to Pittsburgh, leaving me with a sleepless four hours and a locked hotel door. Had I fallen asleep, I would have thought all this was just a nightmare that I dreamed. I thought a heard a noise at the door and ignored it.

I was eating breakfast and reading the newspaper downstairs when Lee joined me. He looked as tired as I felt.

"You warned him didn't you?" Lee said in a low voice while glancing at the menu.

"I had no choice, Lee. You put me in the middle of something that scared me out of my wits. I'm still scared... for both of you."

"Well, maybe it's best this way after all. Just forget everything I told you. Can you do that for me?"

"Yes, I'll be happy to," I lied. I was relieved that he was being so cool. Maybe he had a new plan. Whatever it was, I didn't want to know about it.

Lee stayed in New York for a few more days while Walt and I closed the booth and made arrangements for everything to be shipped back to Pittsburgh. Walt practically ignored me on the flight back. I wasn't sure how much he knew and I didn't feel comfortable discussing any of it with him.

A week later, I learned that Bryan resigned and was also getting a divorce. The divorce shocked me. The

resignation didn't.
A month later, Lee called me to have lunch. He offered me Bryan's job. The money was almost twice what I was making at the advertising agency, and I foolishly accepted. I refused the keys to the Pontiac station wagon however. I felt it was tainted in some way, so they ordered a new company car for me; a white Buick LeSabre. It was beautiful.

Two months after I started working at Hamilton Security Systems, Lee suggested that I get out in the field and work with some dealers. In no time, I was removed from the advertising and marketing activity. Now I was a factory representative, just like Bryan had been, only I didn't play drums, but I was another kind of drummer never the less.

Six months after being in the field, away from the weekly activities at the plant, I leaned that Lee and Marsha were divorcing and that Lee might be taking an extended leave of absence. That took me by complete surprise. The evening in New York was never mentioned and I was happy about that, even though I couldn't forget it. Bryan's trio disbanded and I'd heard a rumor that Bryan had moved to Ft. Lauderdale, where the Bromfield's also happened to have a winter home. Was that a coincidence, I wondered?

"You realize that when Lee leaves, you'll be out of a job here," Walt said. "That shouldn't come as any surprise. After all, Lee was just buying your silence when he offered you this job. You knew that, didn't you?"

Not until that very moment, I didn't. I immediately started making arrangements to get my old job back at the advertising agency. They'd called me a few times and I had kept the relationship friendly.

Over the years I forgot all about that chapter in my life. Then someone had to ask a question, about saving someone's life, and it all came back in a flash.

I wonder whatever happened to Bryan after he went south? I missed not hearing his trio play some of those

Somewhere Along the Way

really cool jazz pieces. Maybe he's still playing gigs and winking at some lady across the room. During one of his breaks he'd no doubt be sitting beside her sharing a cigarette, smiling and waiting for the right moment to return and pick up the beat.

Regardless of where Bryan is now, I'm glad he didn't die that night in New York. Did I really save his life, or just unwittingly take over his position? It's easy to have your judgment clouded when money comes into the equation. It can seduce those with the best intentions.

End

Richard Standring

Shiloh

They advanced into battle,
Not knowing if they would die.
Running, falling, crawling,
Soldiers screaming, crying.

Mortars exploding,
Bullets whistling everywhere.
Cannons belching thunder,
Punctuating their power.

    The sounds of every war!

I hear the echoes of that battle,
Hear the pain of wounded heroes.
See the monoliths now standing,
Where the fighting, dying happened.

Somewhere a distant bugle,
Penetrates the haunting moment,
In memory of all who died here.
Cannons now silent, remain...

    Sentinels to that tragic event!

RAS

Somewhere Along the Way

Richard Standring

Of Days Gone By, and Those to Come

Today's fast pace is a sharp contrast to what life was like just a short 60 years ago. My generation, from The Depression Era, still remembers the quaint sound of a Model A Ford puttering down the road at 20 mph. Also the "Ding, ding" of streetcars, with tracks running in the middle of the street. In 1935, one could drive all week on a dollar's worth of gas. Today, we have faster automobiles, automatic transmissions, cruise control, power everything and pleasure options to entertain us while we speed along at 65+ mph.

During World War II, women went to work in the factories, and that changed our thinking about the workplace and equality. The war imposed many hardships, but those who had survived the great depression didn't feel much need to complain. Housing was a critical item just after the war, when the "Baby Boomers" were being conceived. "Johnny" came home and found a job, and stuck it out for the next 30 or so years until retirement. The company took good care of him and he felt a sense of pride and loyalty for all his efforts. Welfare and minimum wage wasn't part of our vocabulary.

Our family was like most other families when I was growing up. We spent a lot of time at home and with relatives. One of my cousins was like a brother to me. We played together, delivered papers together, and went to church and the movies together. All the aunts, uncles and cousins got together for Easter, July 4th, Thanksgiving and Christmas, as well as weddings, funerals and some birthdays. My Grandmother was the central focus and real strength of our family, and she taught us all well. We loved her, respected her and included her in all our activities. When she died, the family was never quite the same. The aunts and uncles got together occasionally, but never as often, and never all of us.

Somewhere Along the Way

Today, the aunts and uncles have passed away, and the cousins are scattered all over, I don't even know all their names. That's sad. A few of us still keep in touch.

I mentioned delivering newspapers. As a kid, it was a good source for earning extra money. Today, adults deliver papers as a supplemental income because few kids want the responsibility, or because there are too many other demands on their spare time, like soccer games and basketball practice.

When I was growing up, entertainment was playing kick the can, or a game of monopoly with a few friends in the neighborhood. And, listening to the radio. There were a few special programs I would listen to in the dark like: "The Inner Sanctum" and "The Mysterious Traveler" that allowed my imagination to take me to dark, dangerous places. I'm close to the last generation that remembers listening to Jack Armstrong, The All-American Boy, and Henry Aldridge. On Sunday afternoons, I could go to the *show* (movies) and see a double-feature for 10-cents. Popcorn was a nickel.

Later, television came along. Howdy-Doody, and Buffalo Bob entertained my bothers and sisters while Ed Sullivan entertained my folks. Wrestling was my favorite program... on a 12" black & white TV. You had to twist a knob to turn it on, and another to change channels. No remote control, and no color. We marveled at all the progress taking place in our lifetime.

I was just finishing high school when automatic transmissions and air conditioning in cars was becoming a popular option. Buses were still a good alternative, and streetcars were being phased out, even though they were very reliable, and very inexpensive. A ticket was 10-cents, and with a penny transfer, you could ride all over the city with as many connections as you wanted to make. It was time consuming, but nobody seemed to mind. Parking certainly wasn't a problem.

And then there were the wonderful trains. Taking a train to anywhere was a great adventure. It's a shame to see that element of transportation diminish. My last long train trip was from Boston to Seattle while I was in the Army. It took three days, and I loved every minute of it. Years later, I rode the Bullet train in Japan and

Richard Standring

watched Mount Fuji flash by at 150 mph. Looking out the window on the other side, I could see farmers with their entire family planting rice and using oxen... just as their great-grandparents must have done. With progress so close, they continued to live a simple, uncomplicated life. Quite a contrast.

It was the Christmas of 1946 I believe when everyone wanted the new BB ball-point pens just introduced. They were very expensive; about $5.00! Fountain pens remained for a few more years. They are a rare item today, however some executives do prefer them.

I could see that life was changing at a faster pace when more homes were being built with two-car garages. With two cars in the family, there wasn't as much need to stay at home. Driving was an adventure, and my neighborhood expanded to the west side of the city. I no longer needed to go to the local movie theater, I could drive across town, or go to a drive-in. For dating, it was the ultimate thing to do.

Progress took on a new dimension when the phone company announced that the Prospect and Shadyside exchanges were going from the then four-digit dialing to five-digits. To call my grandmother, I had to now dial PR1-8332. Sometimes I couldn't reach her, because she didn't have a private line. It was called a party line so you got a busy signal whenever the party line was in use. And, anyone else on that party line could listen in on your conversation, so you had to be careful what you said. A few years later, the name designations for phone districts were eliminated and push-button phones appeared, soon to be followed by area codes. That series of changes alone told me the world population was exploding.

At the same time, electric typewriters were replacing the old manual models I originally learned on in high school. Today, even the electric typewriters are becoming obsolete in favor of word processors and PCs. Secretaries no longer need to take dictation. Many are now called Administrative Assistants with considerably more activity using office automation. Making color copies was unheard of 25 years ago. And fax machines were just beginning to be used with poor definition.

Somewhere Along the Way

STAR WARS hinted at what tomorrow might be like. We do seem to be accelerating in that direction. The next generations will no doubt spend an hour of designated time playing in the virtual reality room in the basement next to the thermal generator. Meanwhile, Mom will be shopping from her console in the food preparation cubical.

Depression Era babies like myself have been catapulted into the Jet Age and have witnessed technology invade our lives. It is difficult to believe so much has changed in the past 60 years. I've had to accept the change, and make adjustments. While some of the changes have been fantastic, I wonder about the consequences. The family environment isn't the same as it once used to be. Grandmothers aren't sticking around to help teach the grandkids about morals and decency. Instead, they're off to Arizona, or Florida doing their own thing and living much longer with new artificial hip replacements and pace makers.

Modern medicine has allowed us to replace vital body parts and has given us a second chance we would not have otherwise had. Soon there will be a cure for the common cold, and all the current pill and capsule remedies will be replaced with a 10-day patch.

Millions more people now live on the planet Earth than in 1935. Most are living longer, healthier lives. Most are traveling at a much faster pace, too. Slowing down isn't popular, even for senior citizens. Only a few primitive people still remain in remote corners of the world. They must wonder about the giant metal birds that fly so fast overhead, leaving long white trails behind in the sky. Like those Japanese farmers planting rice, perhaps they are more fortunate than they can ever imagine.

Whenever I hear a train whistle now, I stop what I'm doing and listen to the sounds of yesterday. So many memories come rushing back. Then I'm rudely interrupted by my cell phone ringing.

End

Richard Standring

The Men's Room

A humorous short story about attitudes, life and politics in a small southern town whose mayor voted against having pay toilets in public rest rooms, only to regret it later.

Grand Junction is fortunate to have a very active bus terminal. Two different bus lines use this facility. Since Grand Junction is no longer served by passenger trains, it's a convenient way for folks to travel, if they don't have an automobile, or truck. The terminal building is owned by the city. It's a large brick building, located four blocks east of the center of town. On two sides there's a parking lot big enough to hold at least 100 cars. The parking meters were removed three years ago, so now you can park free.

There are meters on the street, but nobody bothers to park there when the bus terminal lot is just as convenient. It's typical of the way the mayor and the town commissioners did things with mixed logic.

The mayor in particular, never thinks about the impact one decision has upon something else, like the time when pay toilets in the bus terminal was a big issue. As a frequent visitor, he was against the idea. So the issue never passed.

Bert Wangerhorst isn't the brightest person in town, but he is, without a doubt, one of the friendliest, and the most frugal. As Mayor for three terms, he knows most of the town's people by sight. Knows their name, and where they live. Black folks all live on the south side. Rich white folks, of which there are only a few dozen, live just outside of town, on the far north side along state

Somewhere Along the Way

route 53. The remaining 11,200 or so citizens live within a grid, with borders on three sides; North, East and West. The commercial district, with warehouses and truck depots, is on the near south side. That's how Mayor Bert keeps all his constituents mentally recorded, by their section.

Mayor Bert's daily routine starts the same way every weekday morning with coffee at the coffee shop in the bus terminal. His coffee is always waiting for him at 7:30. Then he walks down one flight of stairs to the basement where Sam's Unisex Barbershop is located. Mayor Bert gets a shave every weekday. On Fridays, he gets a shoeshine from Old Henry, along with the week's worth of local gossip. Old Henry only shines shoes on Mondays and Fridays.

The men's room is at the bottom of the worn marble steps, next to Sam's Unisex Barbershop. The lady's toilet is on the opposite side of the barbershop. Being right in the middle of all that traffic, Sam added "Unisex" to the barbershop's name about four years ago. Very few people ever noticed the name change. Mayor Bert thought it was a stroke of pure genius. Then again, he also thinks anyone who gets past the 10th grade has made an accomplishment worthy of praise.

"Makes it sound like one of those fancy places where it costs eight bucks to get a hair cut," Mayor Bert offered. He pays fifty cents for his daily shave, and a quarter for the shine. It has never occurred to him to leave either one a tip, so he never has. As a result, it isn't expected. Everyone knows Mayor Bert is a bachelor, still living at home with his aging mother and two cats. Everyone also knows he isn't a highly paid public official. Never the less, it has been mentioned in some circles, that Mayor Bert is, without a doubt, a big cheapskate.

The bus terminal coffee shop is one of the last places around where you can still get a cup of coffee for a quarter, and free refills. Gladys Lafever has been a waitress there for twenty-three years. She always has Mayor Bert's coffee ready for him when he arrives. Double cream with one packet of Sweet & Low sugar substitute. He never tips Gladys, either. Thus, he is able to start every day for just seventy-five cents. And on

Richard Standring

Fridays for a buck, because of the shine. Last year, Gladys took down the sign indicating refills were free. She didn't want to encourage people to sit all day with just one cup of coffee, while waiting for a bus.

Like Mayor Bert, Gladys knows just about everyone who comes into the terminal on a regular basis. A stranger is easily spotted. The breakfast special for a dollar ninety-nine cents brings in a lot of regular customers. As a result, the toilets downstairs also get a lot of traffic.

Mayor Bert is one of those frequent visitors to the men's room. He prefers the middle stall because it is the only stall where the door still has a hook for his jacket. The end stall in the corner has a broken door lock, so he never uses that one, unless the other stalls are out of toilet paper, or occupied. When the TP is out, he reminds Old Henry. "We're out of TP again, Henry," he'll say, embarrassed to be the one to always mention it.

Like so many other bus terminal toilets, Grand Junction's is nothing special, but it is clean. And, it is convenient. In addition to shining shoes on Mondays and Fridays, Old Henry also cleans the toilets. He cleans them every Thursday evening, after attending church services. He is always very busy on Fridays, so cleaning day is Thursday evening.

The local expression among Grand Junction regulars is that on Fridays, you could get a shave and a shine and take a good dump, and still have change left... assuming you didn't leave a tip. It's something Mayor Bert might have said, except he has coffee, too. So for him, the morning costs him a dollar even.

The men's room has three wash basins. Only two have hot water. The third drips cold water only. On the wall behind the basins is a long mirror. For all the years it has hung there, it still remains crack free! Some of the silver on the back has peeled off around the edges, but the main viewing area still puts out a good reflection, thanks to Old Henry's energetic polishing. The mirror is like an old friend. He sometimes talks to it while he cleans.

While there are three sinks, three stalls, and three urinals, there is only one paper towel dispenser. Once a

Somewhere Along the Way

week, Old Henry fills the soap dispensers, fills the paper towel dispenser, replaces all the toilet tissue, cleans the sinks, toilets and urinals, polishes the mirror, and mops the white tile floor. Once a month, he gets out the Ajax and sponges off the graffiti on the stall walls. "It is just downright disgustin' how perverted some folks can be." Old Henry says to the mirror. . "Has to be those transients." Although some of the phone numbers appear to be local.

Old Henry is 78 years old and still has his health. He's been shining shoes at Sam's for 35 years. Nobody can remember what he did before that. In fact, nobody can remember Old Henry's last name, which is Jefferson. His Grand-daddy had been a slave. Old Henry is completely bald. He's been bald since he was 50, so he's always looked old, hence his nickname. A devout Baptist, he goes to church several times a week and never swears, smokes or drinks liquor.

Ruby is Old Henry's favorite niece. However, she's the wild one in the family. And, she is the only one who ever volunteers to help him clean the toilets at the bus terminal. Sometimes when he is 'feelin poorly' Ruby does the cleaning. When she cleans alone, she always leaves the door open and puts out the sign, ***Sorry, closed for kleening.*** The misspelling on the sign has been that way for many years. No one ever seems to notice the error. Ruby is 34 and has never been married, though she has come close a few times. She has one illegitimate daughter, Macy, who will be 14 soon. The second time Ruby became pregnant, she had an abortion. The woman who administered that help charged her $45. The father, doubting that he truly was, refused to pay. The only resulting benefit is that Ruby can no longer get pregnant. This took her awhile to discover, but once realized, she felt free at last. As a result, Ruby relents to her passion for wild one-night stands. The thought of remaining with one man for more than a week is unthinkable.

For a while, Ruby's favors could be had for an evening of drinking at one of the juke joints south of town. Soon she discovered that strangers were willing to pay good money to be with her. So Ruby became self employed. One of her early customers was Deputy Roberts. His full name is Robert Roberts and that is just too much for anyone around to handle. Ruby handles him just fine, however.

Deputy Roberts discovered Ruby's phone number on the men's room wall during one of his frequent breaks. Deputy Roberts is a heavy coffee drinker, as Gladys can tell you. And with the men's room conveniently close, he frequently stops for a quick pee, as Sam can tell you. Very little goes unnoticed by the locals in Grand Junction. It's one of the reasons Mayor Bert leaves town once a month, to conduct some *'private business'*.

Deputy Roberts is divorced. He dated Gladys a few times, but isn't interested in another serious arrangement. His pay isn't enough to support two people, and the prospects for a promotion look pretty slim. After discovering Ruby's phone number, he felt duly obliged to investigate. After that, he inspected the toilet stall walls on a regular basis for new numbers and inspiring messages. Some were actually humorous.

He dialed one number only to discover a man's voice asking if he wanted to meet later in the parking lot outside. Deputy Roberts' sexual preference was limited to women between the ages of 18 and 55. A homosexual experience wasn't a consideration. This did present an opportunity to make a possible arrest on a charge of improper conduct. As for Ruby, the only charge was $ 5.00 for a quick session in his car. He didn't want to be seen going into a motel with her, nor did he want to pay anything extra, much less risk being seen with a black woman. It could jeopardize his reputation.

The gravelly male voice on the phone, refused to identify himself, but did agree to meet him. He waited in the terminal parking lot for two hours looking for an old green '71 Chevy 4-door with a yellow deck lid. It never materialized. Annoyed at having wasted his time, he finally went back to his room at Miss Jean's Boarding House and watched a re-run of "In the Heat of the Night". Grand Junction reminded him a lot of Sparta, the town in the TV series.

A week later, while on patrol, Deputy Roberts

spotted an old green Chevy with a yellow trunk lid on state route 53. He followed the car a few miles until it stopped at a gas station. He pulled along side and saw a middle aged woman with two kids in the car.

"Excuse me Ma'am, may I see your registration please?"

"Why officer? I ain't done nothin' wrong. Just gettin' me some gas is all." The kids were excited seeing a policeman up close and began pointing fingers like guns, "bang, bang, bang", they yelled.

"Yes, Ma'am, I'm checkin' for a stolen car, and this one fits the description. Is this your car?"

"No it ain't. It belongs to my brother. He's workin' so he lets me drive it, so I kin git to the store."

"I see," Deputy Roberts noted the owner's name and the address. Now he knew who the fag was, and how to find him. He wasn't sure what good knowing this would be, unless he was in need of making an arrest, which he seldom did. If Grand Junction resembled the famed Mayberry, then he'd certainly be Barney Fiffe. That thought annoyed him. He preferred to think of himself as casual, yet efficient when needed.

Ruby also inspected the stall walls in the men's room regularly when cleaning. She decided to use the pay phone number at the joint where she hung out regularly. She couldn't use her name for fear Old Henry might spot it, so she selected the name Maybelle. It had a sexy sound to it that she liked. She wrote:

For a hot time, call Maybelle after 9:00. 455-7866

If that didn't work, she had a couple other phrases she planned to try. For the next few nights she sat in the booth next to the pay phone so she could answer it when it rang. She told Sherry, the waitress, that she was expecting an important call and would sort of hang around. Meanwhile, she allowed a few of the locals to buy her a drink, which was all they could afford. The second night, she got her first call.

"I'd like to speak with Maybelle please," the man's voice said in a polite tone.

"May I tell her who's callin'?" Ruby asked, not knowing exactly why.

"Uh, I'd prefer not to mention my name. You see, she's never met me before, and ah... is she there?"

"What you lookin' for Sweetie? You want some lovin' or just some sweet talk?" Ruby was enjoying teasing this guy.

"Okay, sure. A friend of mine gave me this number and said to ask for Maybelle. Said she was real hot stuff."

"You ain't jivin' me, Sweetie! I know where you got this number. It was on the stall wall in the men's room at the bus station, right?"

"Okay, so what? Are you Maybelle?"

"Yeah, Sweetie, I'm your hot mama. You wanta play, you gotta pay, you know what I'm saying?"

"Sure, how much?"

"Depends on what you want to do, and where you want to do it? The meter starts runnin' before anythin' else, you understand?" She hoped she'd make a quick twenty dollars. She was almost broke.

"Uh, yeah, sure. Any chance we could get together tonight?"

"You really got the hots, huh? You want to meet me someplace, or go to a motel?"

"No, no motel. What kind of car are you driving? I'll meet you someplace convenient, but we gotta do it in the car."

"Okay, but I'm not drivin' no car baby, so you gotta come pick me up. You know the south side any?" She said she'd wait outside the joint for him. She was wearing a red skirt, red high heel shoes, and a black sweater. Being on the south side, she didn't have to explain that she was black, too. He should know that if he was a local. If not, it didn't matter, he'd know soon enough.

"Oh shit!" were her first words when she saw the car. It was Deputy Roberts. She hadn't recognized his voice on the phone because he sounded so nervous.

"Ruby! What you doin' here?" he asked. Deputy Roberts was equally surprised.

"Maybelle said she isn't going to make it, 'cause you sounded so jerky on the phone, so I said I'd help her out as a favor, you understand? She's expecting ten dollars though, so I can't do nothin' for five, you know what I mean? You been gettin' it too cheap from me."

"Get your ass in this car, Ruby or Maybelle, or whatever the hell phony name you're usin'. I could bust you for soliciting. You'd spend the night in jail, and have to give it away free to several of the guys on duty. How'd you like that?" Deputy Roberts almost fell for her jive act until he noticed she was wearing a red skirt and red shoes.

"So you still readin' the messages on the men's room walls, huh?" Ruby knew she wasn't going to get anything more than $5.00 from Deputy Roberts. The man was cheap. He had no sexual imagination, either. Every time, he wanted the same thing the same way and that was it. He was proof of her earlier theory, that no one man could ever keep her happy.

"You keep doin' this, you ain't ever goin' to get married. Why don't you get yourself a girlfriend?" she asked, as he drove to a secluded spot in the local park. The police patrolled the park at 11:00 PM and 1:00 AM. He knew the schedule. They had plenty of time, nót that he needed it. He never parked for more than ten minutes. Ruby sometimes thought of him as *Quicky Deputy Roberts*.

"I used to date Gladys once in a while," he said. "all she ever wanted to do was go to the show, walk home, hold hands and sit on the porch. She never wanted to drive or park anywhere."

"That's cause she's smart! She don't want to get in the car with you and be doin' what we're doin'. Lady's smart alright." Ruby meant what she had just said. She felt sorry for Gladys, not having any boyfriend and becoming an old maid. Gladys always had a smile for Ruby.

"Yeah, but all I get for the evening is a kiss goodnight."

"Guess I shouldn't complain. That's what keeps you

boys comin' back to me for some of my special kind of sugar. Now are we just gonna sit here and talk, or are we gonna get it on?"

"How come you wrote Maybelle on the wall in the men's room?"

"Cause I'm lookin' for some new action. How come you be callin' somebody else?"

"Guess I'm lookin' for some new action, too. You want me to drop you off at your house after?"

"Are you crazy? Just take me back to the joint. I may get a call and I don't want to miss it. I can't make any money foolin' around with the likes of you. You wouldn't really throw me in jail would you?"

"Tell you what. You forget about inflation, and I'll forget about puttin' you in jail. But if the price suddenly goes up to say ten bucks, then jail is a distinct possibility." Deputy Roberts knew about Miss Cindy's Cut & Curl. It was a 14 by 70, three-bedroom trailer outside of town. During the day, it operated as a woman's salon. At night, it served as the area's convenient service center for horny husbands who could afford the $15 it cost for a private session. All the commissioners knew about it. Most were clients at one time, or another. Every time Miss Cindy's was brought up for discussion, the commissioners tabled it for later. It had been tabled more than three dozen times. After all, it was just a massage parlor, not a whore house, they snickered knowingly.

"And here I thought we was friends," Ruby said.

"We are. You're the one who wants to make a business arrangement out of it. You used to give it away." The main reason he never saw the need to patronize Miss Cindy's.

"No more, Baby. Freebees are a thing of the past. You want that, you best be gettin' married. Maybe you can get Gladys to put out for you, if you stop bein' so cheap."

"And you think it's free being married? Bullshit! You got to figure the price of a mortgage, furniture, meals out, feeding in-laws, rug rat's dentist bills, and a lot of headaches. No siree, I had that life once, no more. Believe me, it's not cheaper."

"What happened, she dump you?"

Somewhere Along the Way

"Get out of the car, you whore!" Deputy Roberts pushed her out and drove off, leaving her in the park. She had to walk a half mile. It was too far for high heels. Ruby chose to go barefoot, carrying her shoes in the moonlight and singing part of an old gospel hymn. She decided she'd have to try something new on the men's room wall. She also knew she was done foolin' around with Deputy Roberts. She'd touched an old, sore spot.

Mayor Bert's favorite stall in the men's room didn't have any toilet tissue... again! And someone hadn't flushed the first toilet, which he found totally disgusting. He couldn't bring himself to flush for someone else. He used the last stall, taking off his jacket and folding it carefully, he draped it over the stall door, since the hook was missing. That way anyone would know the stall was occupied. Any of the locals would know it was Mayor Bert in there, by looking under the stall door and seeing his black & white wingtips. He wore the same shoes all summer long, regardless of the suit he had on.

Sitting there, Mayor Bert became aware that someone had come in and was using the stall next to him. Obviously they hadn't bothered to check the toilet tissue holder. His smirk disappeared quickly when the smell, and the noise of escaping gas invaded his stall. He expected to hear a flushing sound, but only more flatulence followed. It was a horrible experience! He had to get out of there fast. He was standing before one of the two usable sinks washing his hands, when he heard the flush, then someone called his name.

"Mayor Bert, are you going to leave me stuck in here without any toilet paper?"

He'd been recognized! He didn't know who was in the stall. He wanted to leave, but now he couldn't very well do that and offend a voter. He was running for re-election next year in the primary, and he needed to keep all his voters happy. He went back to his vacant stall and tore off several dozen sheets and passed them over the top of the wall. As he did this he noticed some recent graffiti he hadn't seen before.

Richard Standring

My mother made me a homosexual

Underneath this was scribbled...

If I give her the yarn, will she make me one?

As he rushed out, he heard, "Thanks Bertie". He went upstairs for another cup of coffee, hoping he could get a free refill from Gladys. He put on his best vote-getter smile.

Earl Stompkins drove an 18-wheeler. Mostly he hauled chickens to the packers in Martinsburg. Today, he had a run to Grand Junction, and had a few hours to kill before his return load would be ready. To his friends, Earl was known as "Stomper" because of his size, and because he could take just about anyone foolish enough to challenge him. He liked a good brawl, particularly after he'd had a few beers. Three years ago, he did six months at the county farm for beating up a fag. He couldn't explain it exactly, he just liked to punch out queers. He was 6' 4" and 295 lbs. He had a little gut starting to show, and thinning hair, so he kept it long, like the wrestlers he watched on TV.

Big Earl could spot a fag in a bar, like cops can spot hookers on the street. Sometimes he went trollin' for fags, just for the fun of it. He seemed to attract them like flies on a cow flop. Whenever he thought he'd spotted one looking his way, he'd wink at them and smile. If they nodded, he knew he had another one to mess up. Just thinking about it, gave him a surge of energy.

Big Earl dropped his load at the terminal on the south side. Then he drove his tractor into town looking for a place to park. The only place large enough was the bus terminal parking lot. That worked. He strolled inside to the coffee shop, taking his time selecting a seat at the counter. He wasn't hungry so he just had coffee. Gladys couldn't help staring at him from behind the counter. He was the biggest man she had ever laid eyes

Somewhere Along the Way

on. "Pity his poor wife," she said to herself, looking for a wedding band. She tried to imagine what it must be like to be beneath all that weight. Just the thought of it made her perspire. Gladys gave him her biggest toothy smile, hoping he wouldn't notice her hands shaking as she served his coffee. She almost spilled some.

"Hey Sweets, where's the men's room?" he asked after a few minutes. He was working on a second cup.

"Downstairs. On your right, next to Sam's"

Nobody had ever called her Sweets before. She rather liked it.

Big Earl took his time easing his 295 pounds from the stool. He did everything with a deliberate movement that caused people to take notice. And he enjoyed being noticed. Gladys refilled his cup, hoping he'd return after his quick trip downstairs. She took advantage of the brief absence to check herself in the mirror behind the kitchen door. She dabbed on some lipstick.

Downstairs Big Earl took a leak standing before one of the urinals. As was his manner, he looked around while he peed. He read some scribbles on the wall at eye level.

For some hot action, last stall, 4:00 Wed.

Today was Wednesday, but it was only 3:30. All the toilets were empty. The nervous feeling was starting. He was in a strange town, nobody knew him. So, it would be fun to punch out some local faggot. He'd hang around until 4:00, and see if anyone showed up. He had the time to kill. He went back upstairs to the counter. Gladys noticed he was smiling, and assumed it was because of her freshly applied lipstick. Just the thought of him being interested, made her perspire more. Gladys found she was doing that a lot lately. Either she was going through *the change*, or she was thinking about sex more often. She read all the tabloids and trashy paperbacks at the newsstand by the entrance. She also read her horoscope every day.

At 3:55, Mayor Bert had just left his office, and was walking to the newspaper's office on Elm St. when gas pains hit him. It must have been something I ate at lunch, he thought. The nearest toilet was the bus terminal, a half block away. With luck he might just make it. Having an accident was a deplorable thought.

Meanwhile, Big Earl sipped his coffee... waiting for 4:00. In a few minutes, he'd make another trip downstairs and look aroud.

At 3:58 Mayor Bert rushed downstairs and into the men's room. Not thinking, he went directly to the end stall in the corner. Relief was loud and instant!

About this same time, Deputy Roberts spotted the old green Chevy 4-door, with a yellow trunk lid, parked in the bus terminal parking lot. He also noticed a big Mack truck parked there. He'd never seen that tractor in this lot before. He proceeded into the terminal and down the steps to the lower level, where there was a commotion.

While Deputy Roberts was noting the old green Chevy outside, Big Earl was noting the black & white wingtips showing under the door of the corner stall at 4:00. He'd found his faggot! An uncontrolled urge welled up inside him. In one swift movement, Big Earl pushed open the stall door, which wasn't latched, banging it against Mayor Bert's knees, causing him to yell,

"Hey! Get out of here." Mayor Bert was astonished at the giant facing him, smiling.

Undaunted, Big Earl grinned as he made a fist and propelled it directly into Mayor Bert's upturned face, splattering blood on the stall wall. This evoked another cry from Mayor Bert,

"My God, What do you think you're doing? Help! Somebody call the police! I'm being attacked."

"I'm smashing me another queer," was Big Earl's only reply as he stepped closer.

"Help! Please, please don't hit me again." Mayor Bert was unable to stand up without creating an embarrassing situation. His trousers, and his boxer shorts, were down around his ankles.

Before Big Earl could deliver another blow, a voice from behind him said,

"Hold it right there, Mister, and don't move!" Deputy Roberts was trying to get his handcuffs off his

Somewhere Along the Way

belt, as Big Earl turned around. It was obvious that Deputy Roberts wouldn't be able to subdue this giant. Quickly and awkwardly, he withdrew his revolver catching it on the holster as he pulled upward. This was something he hadn't had to do in the last five years. In his excitement, the gun discharged, accidentally striking Big Earl's right foot. The bullet put a hole in his boot just above the sole line.

"Oh shit, I'm hit!" Big Earl yelled hopping on one foot while trying to hold the injured foot, with both hands. It was a strange sight. Stranger still was Mayor Bert sitting there with his stripped boxer shorts down around his ankles, while he held his face, his nose broken.

"I think I need a doctor," Mayor Bert cried, totally unaware of the small crowd pressing into the men's room for a better look.

By 4:45, Big Earl was behind bars. His swollen right foot was in a massive bandage. He'd been told to keep it elevated, forcing him to lie down. Mayor Bert was being released with a bandage that covered much of his swollen face. Two black eyes were in the process of developing. In a few minutes, if he could still see, he'd sign a complaint against his attacker.

The men's room was closed for repairs.

Mayor Bert's final order had been for the men's room to remain closed, until new stall locks and hooks were installed on all three stall doors. Had he not been so opposed to pay toilets, when the motion had been made a few years back, all this trouble might have been avoided. Mayor Bert had been against having to pay to use the facilities. He wasn't about to carry dimes just for the convenience, and Sam wasn't about to make change for all those requiring it. So the motion never passed.

Jake Hendershot, editor and reporter for *THE CLARION*, was busy trying to sort out the events at the bus terminal men's room. He had several different, conflicting versions of what happened. Deputy Roberts hoped his picture would appear in the story, since he was responsible for arresting Big Earl.

When Gladys saw Big Earl in handcuffs, she vowed

never to speak to Deputy Roberts again. He'd messed up her horoscope. Big Earl had left a dollar tip and Gladys planned to put it under her pillow, later.

On Friday, Old Henry was busier than normal, shining shoes and giving his version of the recent ruckus in the men's room. He was disappointed it hadn't happened on a day when he was working, so he could tell everyone that he saw it all happen. Periodically, he'd giggle at the thought of Mayor Bert being caught with his trousers down around his ankles, with an audience.

Meanwhile, the editor was toying with three different headlines:

Mayor Wants Pay Toilets in All Public Rest Rooms

Mayor Makes Big Stink Over Men's Room Ruckus

Mayor's Nose Out of Joint Over Broken Door Locks in Bus Station Men's Room

End

Somewhere Along the Way

Richard Standring

I'll Tell You What

Having lived in Tennessee for more than twelve years, I've learned a few techniques for blending in with the locals. Like most small southern towns, the people here don't like to hear criticism. Particularly from transplants from other areas. Newcomers are sometimes quick to point out some convenience, they were used to having, that is missing here. That usually prompts a response something like, "Well then maybe you need to move back to wherever it is you came from". If they don't say it, you can be sure they're thinking it.

One of the first big surprises to hit me, when I moved here, was the lack of zoning. Driving down any road I'd see a beautiful brick home in a nice setting, and immediately after, spot an older single-wide mobile home nearby complete with a rusting vehicle with missing parts sitting in the yard. Used automobile tires were scattered on top the metal roof. I learned they're called, "Rumble Buttons". I couldn't help but feel sorry for the people who'd built the brick mansion down the road. On the other hand, the trailer was probably there long before the other folks decided to build their dream home. So they had to know who their neighbors would be before they started to build.

Go just a few miles farther, and you'll probably be confronted with a million dollar view and find yourself admitting that big cities just don't offer such fabulous country landscapes like that. In early spring when the redbud trees start to bloom, followed shortly by the dogwoods, it's a magnificent array of red, pink and white.

Recycling is big in the south. I was never conscious of it when I was growing up in the north. Trash was just trash, and once a week it got picked up. Down here, newspapers and cardboard go into a designated dumpster. The same for plastics, bottles and cans. All get separated of course. And, there are convenient dumpsters in all quadrants of town. While littering isn't encouraged, I see a lot of people along the roadside collecting cans. They probably do it for the exercise. In an effort to help keep the streets, roads and parks clean, the sheriff plans to use inmates to pick up the litter. I like that idea.

Flea markets and yard sales are part of the weekend routine in the south. It helps if you drive a pickup truck because you just never know when you'll see a real bargain. I play golf with a friend who collects, and sells, and trades used golf clubs and riding mowers. Anyone needing a good used riding mower should check with Ken before searching elsewhere. He just loves to trade and find bargains.

You don't need to live here long before you realize that having a garden, even a small one, is the right thing to do. Growing tomatoes and cucumbers helps you start a conversation with just about anyone. Friends and neighbors will give you more zucchini than you can ever eat, so we don't bother growing any.

It is truly surprising what you can grow here in red dirt and clay! Pole beans is another favorite crop you'll find growing in many back yards. The thing that grows best of all is a vine called Kudzu. You can cut it back, but you can't get rid of it! It even grows along telephone poles and guy wires. Someone told me that if you pulled on it hard enough, you'd discover the main root is somewhere in middle Mississippi. I'm told it was imported from South America to help prevent erosion. Too late to send it back.

Local restaurants and small roadside markets frequently offer lunch, buffet-style. You can expect cornbread, iced tea and some variety of beans to be part of the menu along with fried chicken. For breakfast, grits or hash browns come with your eggs. Country ham is a popular side meat. Biscuits and gravy are almost always part of breakfast. For those in a hurry it will be a sausage biscuit. I also learned that everyone in the south eats grits differently. Some like their grits with butter, salt and pepper, which is the way I eat them. Some prefer to mix the grits into the egg yokes. Fried pies are also big in the south. And so is banana pudding (pronounced poodin'). If you have a cholesterol problem, it might be a good *idee* to live elsewhere.

In Middle and Eastern Tennessee, if you drive much, expect to find yourself behind a big logging truck loaded with recently cut trees. Some of these road monsters seem to defy gravity. While you're sure to see the backside for a while, because of all the curves and hills, the upside is you're probably traveling on a well-maintained road. Nothing like the pock-marked roads in the north, where you replace your shock absorbers every other year and get an annual wheel alignment.

Moonshine is still a popular product in the south. I never tasted any *white lightning* while living in the north. Now, I've become somewhat of an expert on the quality of that clear, take your head off, feel it going all the way down to your gut, hundred and thirty proof liquid. Don't forget, Jack Daniels is made in Lynchburg, Tennessee. That was no accident, regardless of what their great advertising says. Old Jack knew a thing or two about corn mash.

Dogs seem to live well in the south. These free spirits can be seen riding in the back of pickup trucks on any given day, regardless of the weather. When they're not in motion, you can find them lying in the middle of some back road, driveway or under a porch. I believe the saying, "leave sleeping dogs lie," originated in the south.

Then there are the hay and tobacco fields. When it's time to cut hay, that becomes a top priority, other important activities just have to wait. The same goes for deer season. It's an unofficial holiday in the south. You're in big trouble if your hot water heater quits during deer season.

Terminology and phrases can surprise you. All the men, regardless of age, will call you, "Son". I even heard a few call me, "Honey". And they weren't being flirtatious. When a waitress calls you "Sweetheart," don't get too excited. She calls everyone by that name. When someone says, "If you don't care (to do something)," they're really saying, "If you don't mind". If you're selling something, expect to hear, "Do you Jew a little?"

Somewhere Along the Way

It's not meant as a racist remark, but rather meant as, "Will you come down from that price?"

I've frequently heard someone ask, "What are you up to?" and the other person usually replies, "Just riding around." even when they're not driving. When someone is surprised, or just can't find the right words, they'll frequently exclaim, "Well I'll be."

And many southern conversations start with... "I'll tell you what."

End

Richard Standring

Where the Sun Always Shines

It had been quite a while since Willis saw his wife, Ann totally naked. Seeing her now, in the buff, came as a surprise, since she appeared to have a very complete tan. No white patches showing... anywhere. For some reason that annoyed him.
"Have you been going to a tanning salon?" He asked.
"Yes, do you like the effect?" Ann had been going twice a week for the past three months, and never once had Willis made any comment, until now.
"Well, I'm not sure you need to be doing that. I liked you just fine before you took to looking more like a Mexican." Willis had seen the flyers that came in the mail advertising specials at The Sun Palace, *where the sun always shines*. Every time one arrived, he promptly threw it away. Apparently he missed one, since Ann was now a member.
"Honey, it doesn't cost that much, and I'm not there very long, just thirty minutes."
"Yeah, but how is it you're brown all over? Don't you wear a bathing suit, or underwear while you're in there?" One good appraising look offered the answer.
"Some people do I suppose, but I don't. Don't worry, nobody sees me."
Her argument wasn't very convincing. The more he thought about it, the less he liked the idea of his wife laying on a mat, or a bunch of light bulbs, totally naked, sunning her buns. With all the perversion he'd read about lately in the newspapers, there could easily be some whacko peeping through a hole in the wall. That thought festered for the rest of the week.
"I don't want you going to that tanning place any more." He stated over dinner on Saturday night.

"Don't you think that should be my decision?" Ann

was surprised that Willis was so upset about her visits. It was something she enjoyed doing, and she liked what she saw in the bathroom mirror. She didn't understand Willis' recent attitude. He had never objected to anything else she did, even when she came home with a changed hairstyle. Working part-time gave her a feeling of independence. Perhaps that's what this is all about, she thought.

"Shoot, we have a perfectly nice deck in the back that's private enough for you to sit out there and get a good tan. Why don't you just do that instead?" It would also be more natural, he wanted to say. He was having difficulty expressing his feelings on the subject.

"Yes I could, but it would take longer, and I wouldn't get as even a tan all over, as I do at the tanning salon. Could we just close the subject and not debate it any more?" She hoped that would end the discussion.

"Okay, but I'm telling you for the last time, I don't like you going there." With that said, he left the house to be alone, and to think about a suitable solution to his dilemma. When he was younger, he might have driven to a local bar and gotten drunk. Now he was older, and presumably wiser. He knew that drinking would not provide the answer he was looking for. If only the Sun Palace would close, or go out of business, his worries would be over.

Three weeks later, the solution to his angst appeared in the local newspaper:

SUN PALACE BURNS, ARSON SUSPECTED

The Sun Palace was totally destroyed by fire Sunday evening. Fortunately the establishment was closed and no one was in the building. There were no witnesses. Fire investigators suspect arson. The owner, Mrs. Caroline Phillips stated that all the tanning equipment was relatively new and in good condition ruling out an accidental electrical problem. Damage is estimated to be at least $ 100,000. No motive yet for the arson.

Sitting on the deck was a new chaise lounge Willis had ordered from the Sears catalog. He was reviewing plans to build a new six-foot high privacy fence for the back yard. And if that didn't do the trick, then his next step was to build a swimming pool. He'd spent the better part of the day removing two huge shade trees in the back yard, so there would be plenty of sunshine now.

Ann arrived home, not noticing the mess of wood chips and branches still in the back yard.

"Honey, guess what? A new health club just opened in town." She seemed excited.

"Oh yeah? You think I need more exercise?" Maybe he could steer the conversation in a different direction. The thought of him and Ann in a romantic clutch, caused him to smirk. Just wait until he revealed his backyard surprise.

"Not necessarily. Mary Alice and I joined today. And guess what else? They also have a tanning room there. Isn't that great?" She saw the smirk disappear.

That's just freaking wonderful, he thought to himself. Now Ann could work out in a room full of sweaty muscle-freaks in skimpy outfits, showing off their bodies... and ogling hers. Things weren't better, they were worse than before, not to mention two good shade trees gone. Jealousy could sure twist a man's thinking. On the other hand, he concluded, the sun didn't have to shine *everywhere*.

End

Somewhere Along the Way

Richard Standring

Bragging About the South

Biscuits, gravy and grits,
'Bout as good as it gets,
When you eat breakfast in the South.

Red beans and rice,
Make's a meal nice,
That's what it's about in the South.

Fried chicken is the best,
Just put it to a test,
You'll agree, it's better in the South.

A secret no more,
They've got places galore,
Cracker Barrels, throughout the South.

Moonshine in a Ball jar,
It's smooooother by far,
Best whiskey is made in the South.

Rebuds first to bloom,
Dogwoods follow soon,
'Cause spring comes early in the South.

Head North, you want cold,
Four seasons there, I'm told.
We only have three in the South.

                                        RAS

Somewhere Along the Way

Richard Standring

The Art of Winning

A short story about arrogance and youth vs. patience and experience in the competitive world of advertising.

Marquis Advertising, one of the top 10 advertising agencies in New York City, was responsible for the Papyrus Group account. Papyrus was the acknowledged leader in cell phones, hand-held computers, laptops, copiers, printers and scanners. Each product line had its own profit center, and product line manager, who was responsible for sales, marketing and advertising. Marquis Advertising provided a separate account manager for each of those product lines, each answering directly to Louis Mark, Chairman, CEO and son of the founder. Their agency's slogan was, *The Marq of Superb Communications*. The agency deliberately misspelled mark for the unique recognition factor.

Jules Papp was the chairman, CEO and founder of Papyrus Group. He started the company in the late 1980s in an old concrete block building in White Plains. The corporate offices now occupy the entire area where that concrete block building once stood. The man was an electronics genius and surrounded himself with similar, but younger talent. Jules Papp was approaching 64, yet he looked considerably younger. All product line managers were in their late 30s to early 40s, and all the product advertising managers were in their late 20s to early 30s. Consequently, the employee parking lot was filled with sporty makes like BMW, Porsche, Lexus and Jeep Grand Cherokee. A first time visitor knew instantly this was Yuppyville.

Somewhere Along the Way

Typical of the high-tech electronics industry, impatience, annoyance and arrogance prevailed among this young aspiring group of executives. Jules Papp, while a modern day legend, possessed none of those characteristics. To the media he was an enigma and illusive. Jules Papp did not seek personal publicity. Only the product line managers had access to his penthouse office on the top floor.

Originally from Philadelphia, Ben Willoughby was living in New York on a temporary basis. He was writing a book about the advertising world in which he'd lived and prospered for over 30 years. To keep all his facts current, he felt it necessary to re-enter the advertising agency scene for a short period. After all, Madison Avenue was still considered Mecca. Roger was staying with his retired brother, who happened to own a nice apartment on fashionable Park Ave. It helped that his brother was also divorced and had a housekeeper.

The problem Ben was having, in his attempt to gain employment, was nobody wanted to hire him on a short-term basis. Agencies also wanted someone much younger. Ben had just turned 60 and was over qualified for most available positions. He started his career as a copywriter. Later, he became an account executive, then a vice president and account supervisor. Just before he retired, Ben had an opportunity to become a partner in a smaller shop. He turned it down so he could return to his first love, writing. Over the years he'd known, worked for, or locked horns with many of the great names in the business, so he had an impressive resume.

Ben's good fortune happened quickly while waiting for an interview at Marquis Advertising. He planned to modify his approach and not mention his quest for work on a short-term basis, or mention that he was writing a book. He was waiting for an interview with the famous Louis Mark, who just learned that his key account manager, Roger Morris was in a serious automobile accident and would be laid up for six months. This was fortuitous for Ben Willoughby. Louis Mark needed someone with experience to fill in quickly. During the interview with Ben, Louis decided not to mention that this might be a temporary assignment.

Roger Morris, who was still hospitalized, was 36 years old, single and quite popular with the ladies. This attribute also made him popular with Lee McKenna, the advertising manager with whom Roger worked closely. Lee was 32 and also single. Therefore the two spent numerous evenings together hitting the more popular singles hangouts. Louis Mark knew Ben would be a considerable contrast to Roger. At the moment, he didn't have anyone else available to fill in, so hiring Ben was an expeditious decision.

Roger Morris had a nice window office on the 16th floor, overlooking Madison Square Garden in lower Manhattan. Because he was expected to eventually return, his office remained vacant. Ben was given a closet-size cubical, surrounded by secretaries referred to as communications assistants. Ben started the same day as his interview and spent the morning learning as much as he could about his new client, Papyrus. From somewhere on the other side of the partition Ben could hear Ricky Martin's Latin beat. While he liked the music, it was a distraction. In the afternoon, he was introduced to the creative director, Hugh Rosenberg and given a quick tour of the Art Department, then passed onto Public Relations on the next floor. Since Papyrus was publicly traded on the stock exchange, the PR people were heavily involved with investor relations. Ben was quick to note that product publicity had a lesser priority.

All of the account managers were out of the office. Ben would eventually meet them. He was scheduled to meet his client the next day, since there were layouts for a new campaign to be presented. Louis Mark announced Roger's accident, and Ben's filling in, with a phone call. He didn't want Ben arriving at Papyrus without some prior introduction. Under normal circumstances, Louis would have gone out to the client's offices with Ben and introduced him personally. Unfortunately, a hectic schedule prevented that from happening.

Ben had forgotten just how busy an agency can be

when new advertising programs are being created. He had jumped back onto the fast track without the benefit of a running start. The fact that he was older than anyone else at the agency wasn't missed. His sandy hair was showing a lot of gray at the temples. His blue pinstripe suit was also in sharp contrast with the casual attire in the office. Even Louis Mark was wearing khaki pants with a tweed sports jacket without a tie. Overdressed and over-qualified, Roger pledged to do whatever it took to fit in. Only the creative director had shown a friendly interest in him. Everyone else seemed to know that he was just filling in for Roger, so there wasn't any interest in cultivating his acquaintance. This rude attitude was just the beginning.

In preparation for the next day's visit to Papyrus, Ben walked into Roger's vacant office and started looking for earlier client contact reports. Within seconds, Roger's secretary/assistant appeared in the doorway.

"Is there something you're looking for in here?" she asked, not hiding her annoyance.

"Yes, I'm the new account manager taking over some of Roger's duties while he's on the mend. I'd like to review the recent contact reports to get a better idea of what I'm facing with the client."

"They're kept on the computer. And since we're networked here, you can access those reports from *your* office." She turned without offering any further help. She neglected to tell him that he'd need an access code. Eventually he had what he was looking for and made a printout. It would keep him busy most of the evening.

That night, back at his brother's apartment, Ben typed pages of notes into his laptop. He was grateful for the opportunity to get back into the hustle, but it also wore him out. It truly was a younger person's game and he readily acknowledged that fact. He was anxious about his reception the next day when he visited Papyrus. It took him two hours to review the contact reports, but only a few minutes to conclude that Roger was entertaining Lee McKenna several times a week, and on weekends! Ben could only guess what Roger's expense accounts looked like. All the contact reports were politically written, with very little negative commentary. Louis Mark was no doubt impressed and seemed satisfied to let Roger work unsupervised.

There were also copies of contacts made by the PR department as well. Their relationship with Lee didn't appear to be as close as it was with Roger. Lee's boss, Nelson Sterling was the product line manager for cell phones, one of the fastest growing divisions at Papyrus. Ben was able to conclude that just about everything the agency developed for the cell phone line funneled through Lee McKenna. He was the conduit and therefore critical to the agency's ongoing relationship. Jules Papp and Louis Mark had been friends for years but the day-to-day activity took place between the two companies at a lower level. It was Roger's mission to keep Lee McKenna happy and informed. That was now Ben's mission as well. It would be youth vs. experience, in one form or another.

    Ben was five minutes early for his 9:00 appointment with Lee McKenna. He was glad he'd left a half hour early, anticipating heavy traffic. The trip took an hour and a half to get there from Manhattan. Since it was a nice day, Ben drove his vintage Jaguar XK150 roadster. By all standards, it was a classic that always turned a few heads. The security guard at the gate instructed him where to park, after calling to confirm that he had an appointment and was expected.

The reception area reminded Ben of a hotel lobby. Three receptionists greeted visitors, gave instructions, handed out security badges and answered questions.

For the next hour and a half Ben was able to count 78 seats and 10 sofas and read all the newsweeklies on the tables. Nobody seemed unduly concerned that he had been waiting a long time, without an explanation. Finally he was paged and told to use a lobby phone. It was Lee McKenna's secretary calling.

"Mr. McKenna will be tied up in meetings all day. He asked that you leave the layouts with the receptionist. He will pick them up later and go over the material when he has time. Someone will get back to you. Check your email later today for any messages."

Ben listened intently for a hint of an apology. None was given. He felt certain Roger would never have suffered this rude treatment. Ben knew it was just a way to establish early on who was in control of the relationship. Carefully replacing the phone Ben made a critical decision. He was new on the account. He could therefore plead ignorance of any established protocol. If Lee McKenna was too busy to see him, perhaps the product line manager, Lee's supervisor, could find a few minutes to meet with him? Ben was already off to a bad start, there was little more to lose, except his temper and Ben knew how to control that.

Nelson Sterling sent his secretary to bring Ben to his office on the third floor. He was curious why Ben had asked to see him.

"As you no doubt know, I'm filling in for Roger, who had a bad auto accident. In the interest of keeping everything moving along on schedule, I thought perhaps you'd like to take an early look at the new layouts, since I'm already here," Ben said.

"Hmmm. That's not the way it usually works here. Has Lee seen these layouts?"

"I'm afraid Lee's tied up today. No, he hasn't seen them yet."

"Okay, let's have a look." Ben could see the man's concern.

As Ben was placing the layouts on a meeting table, Lee McKenna suddenly appeared. No doubt he'd been alerted that Ben had managed to get an audience with his boss.

"Sorry, Nelson. I haven't had a chance to review any of this stuff yet. I thought I left word to leave them. He must have misunderstood my instructions." The young man didn't bother to introduce himself to Ben. His red face was enough to tell Ben he was upset.

"Hello, I'm Ben Willoughby, and you must be Roger Morris." Ben held out his hand in an effort to shake hands. Roger ignored the gesture and walked over to the table brushing past Ben.

"I know who you are. Somebody forgot to tell you

about the protocol here. Everything goes through me first. You don't bother the product managers with concepts and layouts. They only see finished work. So don't ever make that mistake again! Are we clear on that?" The young man's face was still flushed and he was having a difficulty being civil. Nelson's presence no doubt prevented a more heated selection of words.

"Very clear," Ben responded quietly, maintaining eye contact.

"One phone call from me to your boss... and you're history," Lee hissed.

"Okay, cool it, Roger. You made your point. He's new with the agency and probably didn't know you were the primary contact. And since you kept him waiting quite a long time, he wanted to make sure someone at least looked at these layouts." Nelson turned and smiled knowingly at Ben. It was a one-time intercession. Ben acknowledged the comment by nodding.

"People who don't follow my instructions really piss me off." Lee said without looking at Ben.

"Then perhaps you should make that call." Ben said softly while smiling at Nelson. He'd had enough of the younger man's rudeness and posturing. "History has always fascinated me."

"What? Do you know what you're saying? Have you any idea who you're talking to?"

"Yes. Yes, I believe I do. I'm talking to the young man with whom I had an appointment this morning for nine o'clock sharp. I was instructed not to be late, so I left Manhattan early and drove the hour and half to make sure I was here on time, only to wait another hour and a half in your reception area, without any apology. Then I'm told to leave all this material with the receptionist. If that was all you wanted, we could have sent them by messenger service. These layouts require some discussion. We need your input, so if there are changes to be made, we can expedite the process and stay on schedule. The clock is ticking."

"He makes a good point, Lee. Did you really keep him waiting that long?" Nelson was surprised.

"I was tied up." The young man was livid. He was staring at Ben with piercing eyes.

Somewhere Along the Way

"I'm wondering if you would have kept Roger waiting that long. Or Louis, who planned to be here, but like you, he had a conflict. Do you have time to go over these while I'm still here?" Ben was ignoring the earlier outburst and remained calm.

"Look guys, lets not make a big deal out of this, okay? Lee, if you're having a bad hair day we can review everything later, but right now is the best time for me." Nelson was embarrassed by Lee's bad behavior. Just then, someone coughed. All three men turned toward the door.

"Excuse me if I'm interrupting something, I just want to ask this gentleman a quick question." Jules Papp was standing in the open doorway. "Are you driving that beautiful old Jaguar out there in the parking lot?"

"Yes, Mr. Papp. I'm the guilty party." Ben recognized the famous man from an annual report he'd read recently. He'd also been featured in numerous financial and trade magazines.

"You the new man at Marquis? Louis mentioned something about it on the phone yesterday."

"Yes. I'm Ben Willoughby, filling in for the injured Roger Morris. And by all accounts, not doing a very good job of it here today." Ben said this with a slight grin, extending his hand. The two men shook hands and exchanged knowing smiles.

"I used to drive an old Jag similar to that one when I was at MIT. Great way to pick up women."

"It still is," Ben responded. Both men laughed.

"When you're finished here, why don't you stop by my office for a minute. Nelson can bring you up." With that the man turned and quickly disappeared. For the next thirty seconds, the room remained silent.

"Okay, let's go over these layouts and keep this project moving along," Nelson said.

The three men took seats around the table and Ben made some comments about the overall concept being presented. The four layouts involved a variety of photos depicting different activities. "The idea is to maintain continuity. We can use cropped segments of the photos in other pieces later. It's another form of gestalt." Ben looked over at Lee to see if he was following. "Gestalt is frequently used by Pepsi and Coca Cola in their TV commercials. They can run shortened versions later and still get the benefit of total recall."

"Do I look stupid? I know what a gestalt is." Lee replied, much more subdued than earlier. He was making an effort to study the layouts.

"Yes, well I just wanted to be certain we all agreed on the various options this series suggests." Lee closed his briefcase and was ready to leave.

"How is it you seem to know so much about this campaign and you only started with the agency yesterday?" Nelson asked.

"I've been in advertising for the past thirty years in a variety of positions. I've helped create some rather successful programs over the years."

"But nothing recently, right?" Lee was hoping to make a point.

"That's true. Nothing recently, because I took a few years off to work on a personal project."

"Really? Couldn't make it on Social Security, huh?"

"No, it has nothing to do with money." Ben decided not to explain that he was the benefactor of an sizable inheritance and didn't need to work. He was tempted to mention that in addition to coordinating this program, he'd just presented, he also had a few shares of stock in Papyrus, and would probably attend the next stockholders' meeting.

"I guess not having to work explains your attitude here today," Lee wanted to make one more jab.

"Knock it off, Lee. I've heard enough of your sarcastic remarks." Nelson was getting annoyed with him.

"You can hang onto these. I have copies back at the office. If you think of anything we didn't cover here today, give me a call or send me an email message." Ben started for the door. He made no attempt at another handshake. "By-the-way, Lee, if you'd prefer to direct your call to Louis, rather than to me, I'll understand."

Nelson left with Ben. They walked to the elevators and rode to the top floor. When the elevator doors opened, Ben saw another smaller reception area. Nelson was told that Mr. Papp was waiting for them in his office, through the double glass doors. Jules saw them and motioned for them to enter.

"How about some coffee?" Jules motioned to a set table in the corner. When they were seated and testing the coffee, he asked, "So how did it go down there? Get any agreements? Or did you get fired?" He chuckled indicating that he wasn't taking any of what he saw or heard too seriously.

"With Nelson's help, I think we managed to keep things on track."

"Oh I doubt you needed any help from Nelson. Old dogs like you and me know a few tricks on how to handle these younger people. I think it was a good thing to get someone fresh on the account, don't you think so, Nelson?"

"With no disrespect to Roger, I agree. Ben has years of experience under his belt and he seems to have captured what we're looking for. Lee will no doubt make a few small changes to assert his authority, particularly after today's meeting." Everyone laughed understanding the situation.

"So tell me, is that a nineteen fifty-eight model Jag?" Jules asked Ben.

"I see you know your classic cars. Yes it is. It's one of the first XK one-fifties. My uncle bought it new, so it's always been in the family. I only drive it in nice weather, so I can put the top down."

As Ben was leaving, he was once again paged to an interoffice phone. It was Lee. "Don't feel too smug, Pop. Today was only a temporary win for you," he growled.

"For me, a win is a win, regardless of how it comes about. Nice of you to acknowledge it, though." The young snot had to be tolerated, but he'd lost some of his leverage. Ben drove back to Manhattan feeling like he'd never been away from the game at all.

"How did it go yesterday? Louis asked standing by the entrance to Ben's tiny cubicle.
"Okay. For a while there, it was Mr. Important meets Been There, Done That. Jules Papp stopped by and introduced himself at a particularly critical time. Any changes to the layouts should be minor." Lee couldn't afford to stay upset too long without jeopardizing his position, Ben decided.
"I heard Lee kept you waiting. He can be a real shit sometimes. I should have warned you about him."
"That's okay. Jules Papp and I are having lunch next Wednesday. He wants to drive my Jag to some old favorite haunt of his up in the Hudson River valley area around Poughkeepsie."
"No kidding? That's fantastic! Do you realize Roger has been handling that account for two years and never once met Jules. Then you come along and do it the second day on the job. Amazing."
"Yeah. Score one for the old guy." This experience would fill an entire chapter in his book. He might give it a title like, The Art of Winning.
That afternoon, Ben moved into Roger's office. He was standing at the window, enjoying the view, when Roger's secretary appeared at the door.
"Excuse me. Can I get you anything, Mr. Willoughby?" she asked politely.

End

Somewhere Along the Way

Richard Standring

A Special Place

In everyone's life, there's one address, or place, that is always special. I heard somewhere that the definition of *home* was a place, "where you are always welcome and you can come back any time". For me, that special place was 1115 Clark Avenue, on the near west side of Cleveland, Ohio.

My father grew up there, as did all my uncles and aunts. And we lived there right after I was born. We lived there again just after WWII for a few months. By whatever definition, it was definitely our home and the core gathering place for the entire family.

Everyone congregated there for occasions like: Easter, Thanksgiving, Christmas and a few selected birthdays.

The neighborhood was a mixture of American, German, Polish and Slovakian people, some of whom spoke with a distinct accent. The old ladies, wearing aprons and dust caps, or babushkas, could be seen sweeping their porches and sidewalks on any given day. If they didn't say "hello", they at least nodded to you. All the houses were neat and well-maintained. The garages were behind the houses and opened onto one of many alleys. Cars would also line the side streets as there were no driveways. All the houses were spaced close together, usually separated by a walkway and a small patch of grass, or some bushes.

The steel mills in the Cuyahoga valley, not far from the Clark Avenue bridge and my grandmother's house, emitted an acrid smell that I never found offensive, even though I know now that it was definitely air pollution. At the time, it helped identify the area. Whenever I smelled the aroma of steel mills in other cities, it instantly brought back images of Clark Avenue.

Filo's was an indoor newspaper stand and candy

store on the corner of Clark Avenue and West 14th Street. The bus stop was also on that same corner. The smell of newsprint and tobacco was ever present the moment you stepped inside. You could buy a news-paper, a comic book, ice cream, candy and cigarettes there and load up on some local gossip. Filo knew everyone, and what was going on in the neighborhood. It was a fun place to hang out when I was a kid. Filo never minded that we would read his comic books. Just two short blocks away, a nickel could put me in motion towards Filo's to buy candy. I could run there without stopping. It's no longer there, but the fond memory of that place remains.

The house at 1115 Clark Avenue was home to all my uncles and aunts. Grandmother had seven children; five boys and two girls who in turn raised twenty grand-kids. That house was always a special place to each and every one of them. I moved away from Cleveland many years ago, but occasionally I would return to Cleveland, and when I did, I always took time to drive by, and check on the house, even though it was no longer in our family. It was sold after my grandmother died. Yet it was still symbolic of an earlier time, when all the uncles, aunts and cousins got together. The men played poker around a large kitchen table while the women sat in the living room talking and sewing. The cousins played hide and seek, or tried to lure one of the younger members into the basement to scare them.

My memory of the house is quite vivid. It was a tall, narrow two-story house with a wrap-around front porch and wide steps. The entrance was a big oval glass door that opened into a vestibule where all the coats were hung. This opened into the living room. A bay window afforded a good view of anyone walking beside the house, going upstairs.

There was a separate outside entrance to the second floor where there were five light housekeeping suites. My grandmother rented these by the month. They were completely furnished. Whenever I went upstairs, I was always aware of the mixed smells of food and disinfectant in the hallway. The steps going upstairs got scrubbed once a week.

Richard Standring

The dining room was in the middle of the house with the kitchen in the rear. The pantry held great mysteries for me and my cousins. Hidden on one of the shelves in the pantry was a large tin of marbles. They were no doubt won years earlier by some of my uncles. My cousins and I would hunt for that tin then play with those marbles whenever we got together.

At the rear of the house, behind the kitchen, was a small sun porch. This was an important place because hobos used to come by for a meal, which my grandmother always served to them on that sun porch. Later, I learned there was a unique hobo mark on the sidewalk in front of the house so the hobos always knew they could get a hot meal there. They also knew that Mattie, my grandmother, was a widow, and that her husband, my grandfather, was once an engineer with the New York Central Railroad. Consequently my grandmother felt compassionate toward the hobos who would stop for a hot meal. Some would even bring news from distant relatives in Mt. Carmel, Illinois, where she was from originally.

The alley behind the house holds dozens of fond memories. It is where we frequently played and rode our bicycles. Between the house and the alley, there was a three-car garage that obscured the alley from the house, thus grandmother couldn't always see us when we were playing. I think I smoked my first cigarette behind the garage, in the alley. The backyard was small yet big enough for clotheslines and a few rose buses.

The basement was a bit spooky, and frequently damp, since grandmother did the wash down there and sometimes hung clothes to dry, when the weather didn't permit hanging them outside. There was a fruit cellar under the stairs. At the front end of the basement there was a huge coal bin and the giant-size furnace. Every night the furnace had to be banked and several times a day the coal-eating monster had to be fed. I remember shoveling coal from the coal bin to the furnace.

When I was five, I used to imagine that a horrible creature lived down there, waiting to grab me, so I never

Somewhere Along the Way

lingered when left alone in the basement. I always hurried up the stairs as fast as I could go, always glad to have outrun the boogey man hiding down there... somewhere.

The porch and steps was a fun place to sit and watch the passing cars, trucks and busses. Some nights when my Cousin Donny and I would sit there and count the passing vehicles. I'd count all those going east toward the bridge, and Donny would count those going west. He usually won. On summer evenings you could see the glow of the steel mills in the nearby valley.

The memory of that special place remains fresh in my mind. It was a sad moment the last time I drove by and discovered a vacant lot where the house once stood. The lot looked so narrow. It was hard to imagine that big stately house on such a small plot of land. I felt part of the past was beginning to disappear. Just a year earlier, I was looking at the house, and driving down the back alley, while trying to remember the names of all the former neighbors who lived there.

The house was a symbol of another era, when life was much simpler, and you could buy a comic book for a dime, or an ice cream cone for just a nickel... at Filo's, on the corner of West 14th Street and Clark Avenue. It was home, and will always remain *a special place* in my mind, never to be forgotten.

End

Richard Standring

Somewhere Along the Way

Early Lessons

It didn't take long for me to discover that Howard Beesley and I would never be friends. Howard lived just four blocks away, but it might as well have been a mile. The Beesleys lived in a nice bungalow on West 48th Street. It was a quiet, tree lined street. I delivered newspapers to many of the homes in that neighborhood.

We, however, lived in a government housing project where many of the homes were two and four-family units. I'm sure, as I look back on those days, the people living on West 48th Street would have preferred to have "*the projects*" located elsewhere. It was as if an invisible railroad track separated us, and we were living on the wrong side of the tracks.

For most 14-year olds, including me, bicycles were a primary means of getting around. I rode an old, no name single-speed bike that I painted green. Howard owned a coveted red Schwinn with lots of chrome. I thought it was the most beautiful bicycle ever made and wished I owned one just like it.

What Howard and I had in common was Shirley Anderson. The Andersons lived about half way between us on West 50th Street (close to where those invisible tracks would have been). The Anderson's house had a big front porch with a swing and wide steps. It was a great place to hang out, particularly since Shirley's mother baked delicious oatmeal cookies, which she graciously offered to all the visiting kids in the neighborhood. It was also a favorite stop on Halloween.

I recall frequently dreaming about Shirley. I also had dreams about riding Howard's red Schwinn, which appeared too often, to suit me, in Shirley's front yard. Competing for Shirley's attention was difficult. She had a lot of friends and was popular in school.

The growing friction between Howard and me

culminated on Shirley's 14th birthday. Her mother must have invited at least 100 kids. At least it seemed that way. Howard and I had a brief glaring contest, occasionally elbowing each other on our way to the refreshment table. There was punch, cookies and a birthday cake.

I remember I brought Shirley a box of Whitman's chocolates, which she promptly opened. She sampled one, and with her mouth still full of candy, kissed me on the cheek. I felt my face burning and knew that everyone in the world was watching. Then Howard gave her a bouquet of summer flowers and received a similar kiss. My burning face remained and now I also had a churning stomach, as I watched with a growing annoyance.

While Shirley was putting the flowers into a vase with water, Howard sauntered over to the open box of candy, selected a piece, then accidentally bumped the box off the table, spilling the contents on the floor. I think Howard even managed to step on one before Shirley's mother promptly removed the mess.

I knew it was deliberate and considered removing the flowers and emptying the vase on Howard's head. However, I knew that would never come off as an accident, and I would appear to be the jealous one. I had to think of something to get even, without Shirley imagining how I truly felt. Jealousy, envy and anger are difficult emotions to juggle along with puppy love. All of that was going on with me when Howard suddenly stepped up behind me.

"Hey stupid, why don't you have another big helping of cookies and then beat it," he whispered.

I was at the refreshment table. Howard was directly behind me. My hand was suspended, holding the fruit punch ladle half full of punch. As I abruptly turned toward Howard, fruit punch somehow managed to drench the front of his shirt. It happened so fast. The next moment, Howard was pushing me and yelling, "You did that on purpose!" Several girls were giggling.

The next moment found us both in the front yard surrounded by everyone in the world. I didn't want to fight with Howard, even though I was angry. Before I knew what was happening, he hit me in the face momentarily stunning me.

Somewhere Along the Way

"Fight, fight!" several kids yelled.

My anger grew and I realized my only option was to fight Howard, or look like a coward. My face hurt and I could feel tears running down my cheeks. I hated having Shirley see me crying. For some reason, I stepped back holding my hands up in a surrendering posture. My father once told me that when you did this, your opponent was sure to move in, feeling confident and thinking you would be easy to finish off. I must have looked like a coward as Howard gave me an ugly smirk and moved in to place a well-aimed punch. He threw a wide swing meant for my head, planning to knock me to the ground.

This time I was prepared. I quickly side-stepped his fist, caught his arm with both hands and swung him around hard. The momentum forced him to lose his balance and he fell. Once on the ground, and a bit surprised, I took quick advantage putting a knee into his ribs. He tried to stand, staggering backwards, giving me the perfect opportunity to punch him in the nose. I put all the energy I had into that punch. Howard's nose began to bleed profusely. Blood was dripping all over Howard's shirt. Now it was Howard who was crying.

The fight was over by the time Shirley's mother arrived to break it up. She took a quick look at Howard and admonished me, telling me to leave.

While Howard's nose wasn't broken, my heart was. From that day on, Howard and Shirley became close friends. He had Shirley all to himself... along with that beautiful red Schwinn, with all that chrome. I hated him!

A few weeks after the fight, my father gave me some advice, "You don't always get everything you want," he said. Somehow, he must have known what I was feeling because soon after that, we found a used Cushman motor scooter for sale, elevating my spirits and local status, and expanding my neighborhood horizon.

I also rode that baby up and down West 50th Street every chance I had. Somehow Howard's beautiful red Schwinn, with all that chrome, wasn't so important.

End

Richard Standring

"Ask Your Doctor About...."

If you watch television, even for a short period of time, you've been bombarded by a series of medication commercials that start with, "Ask your doctor about...
**Albuterol"
Allegra"
AstraZeneca"
Celebrex"
Enbrel"
Gaviscon"
Levitra"
Lipitor"
Nexium"
Plavix"
Pravachol"
Prevacid"
Pulmicort"
Viagra"
Vioxx"
Zocor"**

Television commercials and magazine ads for prescription medications, seem to have intensified in the past year. For most of these Greek, or Latin sounding names, I don't have a clue what they're designed to remedy. Most of the names I can't even pronounce correctly. I suspect some help reduce the risk of a heart attack, or they help lower your cholesterol. I think one of them is for those suffering from painful arthritis, but I'm not sure which one it is. I'd have to ask my doctor, I suppose.

Most of my senior friends are talking about Viagra. I have some awareness of what that is supposed to do. Based on the television commercials, seeing all those smiling faces, I gather it's supposed to help put a smile

Somewhere Along the Way

on your companion's face. So I assume it's a remedy for depression. I could be wrong, I haven't asked my doctor about it, yet.

Not too long ago, I recall the war on television to convince us that Tylenol (which contains Acctaminophen) was a better pain reliever than aspirin or ibuprofen. Then Aleve came along. I'm still not sure which is better for a headache and muscle aches. I'd better watch for the commercial, and watch someone impersonating a doctor, show me a graph on which one starts working quicker.

Granted, these are non-prescription items that we don't have to ask the doctor about. You can just read the labels or ask your pharmacist, which is best for you. I think the price is about the same in Canada, too.

Somewhere near the end of these new commercials, the voice announcing the wonder medicine speeds up and proceeds to unravel a lengthy list of possible side effects. That's enough to scare most intelligent people, making them wonder if the trade-off is worth it.

If I actually asked my doctor about any and all of these products, he'd no doubt tell me to stop watching so much television.

For anyone who *must* take one of these new miracle remedies, I understand they are quite expensive. The price must be way up there since this new commodity of wonder remedies is rapidly adding to the Canadian economy. It begs the question, did you ask your banker for a loan, (before ordering your prescription)?

The more I think about it, maybe I'll ask my stock broker... about investing in pharmaceuticals. That's something I'd probably understand.

End

Richard Standring

Do the Math

    Billy Giles was out of work again. Friday was his last day at the Z-Tec plant where he'd been a maintenance man for ten months. His supervisor explained there was a reduction in support staff, and those with the least amount of time, were the first to go. Billy was ready to quit anyway, so the news didn't take him by surprise. He'd miss the benefits. The company gave him two weeks paid vacation as a severance. That translated to two weeks of doing nothing before he had to start looking for another job.
    Before Z-Tec, Billy worked at a fast food restaurant for six months. He was fired because he showed up late for work too many times. The silly high school part-timers annoyed him. And, the thought the manager was a dork.
    Working at a local car wash was another bummer, he'd lasted four months before he told the owner where he could put the dirty towels. It was hard work for little money and the tips were split too many ways to amount to anything. Before leaving, Billy managed to switch the hoses for the rinse cycle so that they would apply more soap instead. It was petty prank, yet it gave him some personal satisfaction, knowing a few vehicles would have to go back through the system again.
    Pool maintenance was the best job he'd ever had. He worked outside at a leisure pace and frequently ogled the ladies lounging outside in skimpy bathing suits. Most ignored him. A few didn't bother with their tops causing him to momentarily forget what he was doing. It was difficult to concentrate in those situations. It was his bad luck to be chatting up one young lady when her old man came home unexpectedly, catching Billy's eyes pasted to his wife's totally naked chest.
    The short time he spent working for a moving company hardly counted. It was hard work lugging

boxes and furniture up and down stairs, rarely taking a break. He did manage to break a few pieces of furniture however, which the manager deducted from his pay. The net result was he'd worked for almost nothing. Live certainly hadn't been fair to Billy.

Somewhere, there was a good-paying job waiting for him. He just had to find it and that meant being in the right place at the right time. He felt certain his luck was about to change for the better.

He still had a week to go before looking for another job. Billy told everyone he was on vacation and that's exactly how it felt. While working on a second beer in The Paradise Lounge in the early afternoon, Billy overheard a conversation in the booth behind him. Billy was sitting at the bar alone pretending to watch a soccer game on the TV over the bar.

"Okay, so who do we get to drive the truck?" One of the booth occupants asked.

"How about Maria? She's a pretty good driver isn't she?" Another occupant replied.

"Nah, she ain't gonna get involved. I'm keeping her out of it."

"Yeah, you're probably right. Once we get everything organized, we'll be wondering how to spend all the money."

"Hey, I think that guy at the bar is listening. Hey you, yeah you over there. Come here."

Billy turned around, saw one of the three men motioning to him. The three men all looked to be in their late 30s or early 40s. There was no law against listening in on someone else's conversation, so he had nothing to worry about. He walked over to the booth. "Something you want?" he asked, trying to look uninterested.

"Yeah. How 'bout you move your ass to the other end of the bar, so you can't hear us talking over here. We're having a personal business conversation and it doesn't involve you. You get my drift?"

"Does that mean you're buying me a drink?" Billy asked.

"Yeah, sure. Have one on me and get lost."

Billy did as he was told and moved down to the far

end of the bar. He was pretty sure they were planning to hold up a bank somewhere. They needed a driver and they were planning to use a truck to pull it off. One of the guys had a girlfriend named Maria and he didn't want her to get involved. That was as much as he'd been able to piece together before being asked to move.

That night, Billy had a wild dream. In it, he was driving the getaway truck. Actually it was a van with a moving company logo on the side that looked very familiar. Billy was behind the wheel, the engine running and the driver's side window was all the way down. Billy was checking the side mirrors making sure no one pulled in and blocked him. He heard the alarm go off, then shots were fired. Two of the holdup guys came running around the corner and jumped into the rear of the van.

"Move it!" One of them shouted at Billy.

"Where's the other guy?" Billy asked pulling out into traffic. He cut off an oncoming automobile and heard his horn blaring in protest.

"Dead, and you will be too if you don't goose this thing. I thought you knew how to drive."

Turning his head, Billy could see one of the two men was bleeding. He'd been shot. The other man was attempting to count the money they'd just taken. He was stacking the bills into two piles.

"Don't forget my cut," Billy yelled over the racing engine. He had to be careful not to get pulled over for speeding.

Suddenly a car swerved in front of the van causing Billy to jam on the brakes to avoid hitting the other vehicle. The man counting the money fell forward hitting his head hard. He appeared to be unconscious. The bleeding man was having a difficult time stopping the blood. His shirt was soaked. Billy couldn't see where he'd been hit, but it looked bad. The money was scattered all over the floor, some of it had blood on it now. Billy saw a shopping center parking lot and pulled around to the back of the building where other trucks were unloading merchandise at docks. Billy was pretty sure the bleeding man wasn't going to make it. Now he had to contend the other man still unconscious. Billy found the fire extinguisher and hit the unconscious man on the head as hard as he could. The bleeding man didn't seem to notice.

Crawling into the back, Billy scooped up all the money and put it back into the briefcase. He found a mechanic's wiping rag on the floor and wiped the fire extinguisher, then the steering wheel, door handle and the key, which he left in the ignition. He kicked the door closed and walked away from the parked van, hoping not to be noticed.

He was still counting the money at his mother's house when the police arrived. He had no idea how they found him. The next scene was the judge sentencing him to ten years in jail! The stolen money amounted to $5,500.

"Do the math, Son. It comes out to five hundred and fifty dollars for each year," the judge said. "You'd been better off washing cars." Billy was handcuffed and taken away.

He woke up in a sweat. Those guys back at the bar needed to do the math. It wasn't worth it, regardless of how much money they stole.

Billy decided that same morning to look for another job. The vacation was definitely over. Any job that promised a decent future would be satisfactory. It was time to start thinking about the future and not just take things one day at a time as he'd been doing.

Later that same day, Billy stopped at the Paradise and asked the bartender about the three men who'd been sitting in the booth the day before.

"Those three are starting a catering business. I hear they're looking for a driver. You interested?"

End